Living with the Sermon

Living with the Sermon

Signposts on the Footpath of Preaching

Robert P. Hoch-Yidokodiltona

▲ CASCADE *Books* • Eugene, Oregon

LIVING WITH THE SERMON
Signposts on the Footpath of Preaching

Copyright © 2024 Robert P. Hoch-Yidokodiltona. All rights reserved. Except for brief quotations in critical publications or reviews, no part of this book may be reproduced in any manner without prior written permission from the publisher. Write: Permissions, Wipf and Stock Publishers, 199 W. 8th Ave., Suite 3, Eugene, OR 97401.

Cascade Books
An Imprint of Wipf and Stock Publishers
199 W. 8th Ave., Suite 3
Eugene, OR 97401

www.wipfandstock.com

PAPERBACK ISBN: 978-1-4982-2565-6
HARDCOVER ISBN: 978-1-4982-2567-0
EBOOK ISBN: 978-1-4982-2566-3

Cataloguing-in-Publication data:

Names: Hoch-Yidokodiltona, Robert P., author.

Title: Living with the sermon : signposts on the footpath of preaching / Robert P. Yidokodiltona.

Description: Eugene, OR: Cascade Books, 2024 | Includes bibliographical references.

Identifiers: ISBN 978-1-4982-2565-6 (paperback) | ISBN 978-1-4982-2567-0 (hardcover) | ISBN 978-1-4982-2566-3 (ebook)

Subjects: LCSH: Preaching.

Classification: BV4222 H55 2024 (paperback) | BV4222 (ebook)

VERSION NUMBER 09/03/24

Revised Standard Version of the Bible, copyright © 1946, 1952, and 1971 National Council of the Churches of Christ in the United States of America. Used by permission. All rights reserved worldwide.

Gwendoline N. Hoch, "Three Peaks of Yorkshire," and "Curlew" reprinted by permission.

Imogen E. Hoch, "Dancing Ravens," "Footpath Sign," and "Tsimshian Mask" reprinted by permission.

Jack Baumgarten "Walking Man of the Burden," reprinted by permission.

To Gwendoline

Solvitur ambulando

Contents

Acknowledgments | ix
Introduction | xi

Part One: Callings
Chapter One   A Peek and It Winks Away | 3
Chapter Two   Unfit for Preaching | 20
Chapter Three   Haunted like Holy Things | 35

Part Two: Tinkering
Chapter Four   Creature Comforts | 53
Chapter Five   Wooden Tongue | 71
Chapter Six   Coloring by Numbers | 90

Part Three: Community
Chapter Seven   Wee Gaggles | 113
Chapter Eight   Difficult Journeys | 128
Chapter Nine   Distance Walking | 144

Conclusion | 167
Bibliography | 169

Acknowledgments

WHILE SOME PEOPLE MAY be able to write books alone, I am not one of them. Throughout this work, you will meet people who have supported the progress of this work, some directly and others only indirectly but no less significantly. As such, gratitude must always remain partial, incomplete, and thus continuing as in vocation.

In that spirit, I owe a debt of gratitude to the editors and support staff at Wipf & Stock, who were invariably helpful and patient with me during the writing process.

When I joined the Urban Theology Union at Sheffield in July 2021, their book writing group gave me a physical deadline, reinforced by face-to-face conversation about my work in the basement of Victoria Hall Methodist Church in Sheffield. Beyond the deadline, those meetings encouraged me as I heard seasoned preachers, particularly with the Reverend Drs Ian Duffield and Robin Pagan, warm to this conversation about the art of preaching, an activity as familiar as their own homes and memories. Similarly, the ministers and lay preachers serving the North Western Synod of the United Reformed Church gave me a sense of "who" I am writing for—during the course of writing, I often asked, "What will help the preacher in their journey?" Their vocations and the unique challenges of preaching in a dynamic and changing environment shape much of what I have written here.

I am also indebted to early readers of this work, including the Reverend Daleen ten Cate, who read an early draft of this work while living in a shepherd's hut on a personal walking retreat, an apropos setting for this kind of reading. Sharing a work like this with a colleague like Daleen is a wonderful gift in itself—and, as you might expect, my work grew because of her insights and questions.

Acknowledgments

A former student, Reverend Dawn Helton-Anishinaabeqwa, who always taught me more than I ever taught her—her modesty wouldn't let her admit that, but it's true—dove into my manuscript while moving house. Amid the dust and detritus of moving, of boxes and evaluation of what we take and what we must leave, she quickly identified where things were overgrown or needing to be freighted off for another day. If you sense that I've gone on too long, that is entirely the author's responsibility—I was warned!

And, not least, my companion on the footpath of life, Rebecca. In our life we have shared footpaths in Alaska's Denali (the "Great One") and with the Tsimshian of Metlakatla on Queen Annette Island. After children came, the footpath took us through Swiss Valley of Iowa, and later through Baltimore's Druid Hill and graffiti alley, and during the summer months on miles of trail through the Shenandoah Mountains of Virginia (the "Daughter of the Stars"), and in England, our second home, on footpaths in and around Yorkshire, Lancashire, and throughout the Lake District, even to the point where we nearly drove our entire family into the North Sea as we looked for the Boggle Hole Youth Hostel. These ordinary adventures (and near misses) have enriched my life immeasurably.

Our oldest daughter, Gwendoline Nenana, takes a different path beginning in August 2023. She'll be living in LA, the City of Angels, where she'll be starting university. I'm dedicating this book to her, to the place she will call home for a while, to the people she will call friends and companions:

> May the road rise up to meet you.
> May the wind be always at your back.
> May the sun shine warm upon your face;
> the rains fall soft upon your fields and until we meet again,
> may God hold you in the palm of his hand.

Introduction

My love of the preaching moment was not born in homiletical theory. It was in the moment, the thing that I don't understand and in the experience that turns my best efforts into beautiful failures. It's not easy writing a book on failures, their beauty notwithstanding.

Why I have bothered with this book is because occasionally I've gotten some glimpse of God in the preaching moment—and perhaps that will be of help to someone who, like me, has chosen or been compelled to live with the sermon. John-Paul Flintoff's poem "The Integrated Self," in his illustrated collection entitled *Psalms for the City*, explains why he writes poetry, why he draws pictures:

> How to describe the indescribable?
> And why even bother?
> All the descriptors in the world
> Can't show the infinite.
> Perhaps the best we can do is offer
> A different way of thinking.
> Baffle, instead of rationalize,
> Like with one-hand clapping.
> In daily life, you see a person laugh, cry, shout
> but never all at once.
> You never see the whole, integrated self.
> God's a bit like that.
> I only see God's footsteps,
> Catch a heel as it disappears up the hall.
> And contemplating this brings peace.
> That's why I bother.[1]

---

1. Flintoff, *Psalms for the City*, Kindle ed. loc. 447.

Introduction

I don't think I could come up with a better way of saying why I bothered with this meditation on the preaching life. I draw pictures, mostly with words. My daughters have added some of their drawings to this work, their better word. When they added those drawings to my words, they restored my energy for this book; the work came to life again. I hope their drawings will do that for you, too. Talking to a friend about what a reader might find here, I said I might need to warn them about the word pictures—about prosthetic tongues, like one-hand clapping—that things like this might "baffle" in a book about preaching. Curious as it sounds, a wooden tongue is oddly clarifying for something in preaching that I can't fathom or properly describe otherwise.

So, yes, you will read about prosthetics, and manuscripts, commentaries, and birds pecking at seed, and of a dog long since dead nipping at our calves as we turn east on the coast-to-coast path across England. Our path will zigzag one way and then another, but through the many things of preaching, I will try to convey a sense of its depth. The art of preaching feels like a hybrid medium, the ephemeral and the mysterious co-existing. James K. A. Smith introduces an essay on Jacques Derrida in a similar spirit: "Things I think about when I'm paddle boarding [on Lake Michigan]: Jacques Derrida, freshwater sharks, negative theology, cardiac arrest, Rothko's chapel in Houston, mysticism, lunch." The philosopher gathers the ephemeral and the mystical, the connection or the limit experience of something transcendent and the way the ordinary comes to be a sacrament, as clue or invitation by way of the visible sign of an invisible presence. According to Smith, if "God" is the word we use for "limit" then we might feel haunted by the holy—but these thoughts were not at the desk, but while "paddle boarding on Lake Michigan."[2] Paddle boarding on Lake Michigan, thinking about God or monster, lunch, and the faint warning of cardiac arrest feels about right to the preacher who lives with the sermon. We do not know whether, if the numinous appears, it will swallow us or carry us up into heaven. We cannot know, ever. If we do know, we do not know God, but something else not worthy of the name. We only trust that this One holds us and, for the time being, lets us cling to our paddle boards while suspended over deep places.

This book or my life has felt like this, hovering over a complexity that I don't understand. Drawn to it, at times, against my will. When Dietrich Bonhoeffer was in prison, he spoke of the mystery and love and the

---

2. Smith, "Of God and Monsters," para. 1.

Introduction

sweetness of Christ but he also asked for tobacco ration cards, a beloved book, or a pair of trousers. He enjoyed the gifts of food in prison, reminders of life held with care and kindness. Bonhoeffer lived in a place that was alternatingly monstrous and, by some terrible grace, life-giving—he was able to explore that for us. Yet Bonhoeffer, as close to a saint as a Protestant can ever get, did not go without creature comforts that ordinary people need.

I've looked over the things I've collected in my preaching life, tried to pick out what felt fit for purpose; I've also tinkered with some things that we need to carry along but perhaps they need some readjustment for the footpath rather than the classroom or the academic library. What you find in this meditation on the preaching life will not be as intimate as your backpack or your walking stick and nowhere near as important as your companions. But as a walking-tour guide, I try to give you a taste of the fun, life, and mystery of preaching alongside some advice and recommendations, the homiletical equivalents of "where to stop to get something to eat," sights you don't want to miss, and perhaps a little insider advance on the road ahead—including warning you about a by now long dead farm dog that you'd do best to avoid if at all possible—though I'm sure it is *not* possible.

I love the mystery of preaching and, at the same time, believe that "signposts" (like the security of a paddleboard) can free us to be in the depth of that moment more fully. If we have a sense of the path, how to walk it and where it's taking us, we can enjoy the beauty more readily and freely. So, maybe think of this book as a map with some notes on the side. At best, I hope this meditation on the preaching life will take a beating in the weather of congregational life; I hope that as with any good map, you will find alternative routes and make discoveries of your own. I hope that sometimes it will lead you right or help you get unstuck. I hope that, from time to time, you will pull it out of your pastoral backpack of memories, before stowing it away again, as you plunge into your calling.

I've styled this book as something along the lines of a walking-tour guide. But maybe it's a bit more than the *Lonely Planet*. Ours isn't a lonely planet, or so I believe. Ours is a world God so loves. As one who, like you, has experienced God on the way, I am giving you this book as a companion to your preaching life, as a practically minded partner to a mystery, as an on-the-ground guide to help you navigate the journey from pew to pulpit and back again.

Wherever this short journey eventually takes us, I promise to keep the mystery of preaching in sight or at least in the mists of our thinking.

PART ONE

Callings

Chapter One

A Peek and It Winks Away

"Tell me and I forget. Teach me and I remember. Involve me and I learn."
—Benjamin Franklin

ONE PART OF ENGLAND'S Coast to Coast (C2C) Walk takes you through the Yorkshire Dales National Park. The landscape unfolds around you with long rolling hills of moorland, a sharp change from the Lake District peaks and valleys. We had begun to feel the monotonousness of the path weighing on us. The map told us we were going the right way, but the land told us we were going in circles. Muted daylight had merged into a neutral gray mist with a constant drizzle. It was getting on to noon and we were looking for a pub, the Lion Inn, one of the oldest in England, according to our guidebook. It would be along our path, an old railway for a long-defunct mining industry. At one time this area would have been a hub of activity, now it was mostly the haunt of walkers like us. Like most road-weary travelers, our eyes peered longingly toward the seemingly shapeless horizon, looking for some sign of the Lion Inn.

As we made our way along the railway trail, we saw a crumpled-looking shape alongside the path. We couldn't make it out but, as we drew closer, we saw that "it" was a silver-haired man of about sixty or so years of age. He was sitting on top of a flat rock to enjoy a cup of tea, resting a moment before continuing his walk. When we met him, it felt as if we were the only three people in the world:

"So, you'll be walking the Coast to Coast?" he asked. We nodded. "Then I expect you'll be looking for the Lion Inn?"

Our ears perked up because he knew, the way a walker knows, exactly what we were feeling at that moment. And then he told us what to look for: "You're not far," he said. "Just stay on the way you're going and as you come over a hill, it'll peek at you and then, as you go down into the bottom, it will wink away. You can't miss it: a red roof."

We were relieved: he'd not only given us *directions*, which we probably had in hand well enough, but he had related an *experience*, grasping at an intuitive level how the landscape seems to shift from the walker's perspective. And sure enough, about a mile or so down the trail, the distinctive red roof of the Lion Inn "peeked" at us and then "winked" away as we walked along the contours of the moor. As a fellow traveler, one who had walked this trail many times, he understood not only that we would be looking for a landmark but also how it would appear from our perspective. He spoke in a manner that was not only informative but also reflective of the experience itself.

Companion on the Footpath of Preaching

If I were to choose an image for myself, it would probably be as a companion on the footpath of preaching. I write as someone who frequents the sermonic path: I recognize many of the experiences, joys, and pitfalls of preachers. I've experienced the highs and lows of the preacher. I am also a homiletician. As a teacher of preachers, I've spent a lot of time relating different sorts of paths to the sermonic moment and relating the work of preaching to other theological areas of thought.

That means I am a bit of an odd duck among preachers and homileticians. C. S. Lewis says that teachers know their subject with great depth: they bring to the classroom an encyclopedic knowledge. Why would that be a problem? Because teachers often struggle to hear the questions of their students through the thicket of their expertise. Not long into my teaching vocation, I experienced this firsthand. It was an introductory course in worship. Worship, it struck me, was an intensely cultural phenomenon, drawing on hermeneutical, theological, and biblical resources. Fascinating. Layered. Rich. It was all that and then I read one student's understated, and

A Peek and It Winks Away

in hindsight incredibly generous critique of the course: it would have been nice, she said, if we could learn how to put together an order of service. Of course. An order of service. Yeah, that would be nice, wouldn't it? A service of worship seemed so obvious to the student but an afterthought to me, a teacher. Right at that moment, she was looking for a trailhead to begin the whole journey. I went back to the drawing board, as I tried to recover something of where my students were and what they might need at that moment.

(And worked in cultural hermeneutics whenever I could!)

Maybe there's something of that in this book, something like me going back to the drawing board. Not to erase everything an academic theologian teaches, but to give words and expression to the experience of those who take the footpath of the preaching life. I've got some good company. Augustine quips that if you want to learn how to preach, you should stay well away from homileticians! Some may nod at this—maybe a homiletician's style of preaching resembles the hairstyles of hairstylists—an exaggeration of some ideal towards which we aspire. And yet, here's an irony: Augustine, who was skeptical about rhetoric, also wrote what scholars consider to be the very first book in homiletics, Book Four of *On Christian Doctrine*—and in it he makes a cautious argument for a Christian rhetoric. By this time, Augustine was no stranger to the art of preaching. And yet, he wrote as a theologian, as someone who cared about the integrity of the art itself, like a homiletician who is sensitive to the theology of proclamation and the challenges of communication.

When I originally conceived this book, I was serving as a faculty member in a seminary, had tenure, had published my first book. One of the members of my doctoral thesis committee told me that I was now "established" in the field of homiletics. Somehow, I found that deflating. In 2016, I said yes to a calling in an urban congregation. While I told myself—and anyone who asked—that this was a natural transition, I found that this was only partially true. In the summer of 2017, Princeton Theological Seminary invited me to lead two seminars for newly ordained pastors on the topic of preaching. At the time, I'd been in a full-time pulpit for just about a year. The students were, in most cases, in their second year of ministry. All of us were coming off a particularly turbulent year in America's political life. As we talked, I felt unusually close to their experiences and questions. Do we incorporate "trigger warnings" for talks that might recall potentially traumatic experiences for some in our congregation? Why is it important for White people to talk about whiteness? What are the obstacles to that

Part One: Callings

conversation? How do we, as pastors in a caring vocation, also minister in a prophetic key? Although I wouldn't name it until later, I was experiencing a kind of liminality, being a teacher and a student simultaneously or neither one completely. All this is to say that I have some maps, the maps you might expect to find in the baggage of a theological educator and some of the experience that preachers will recognize as well.

Ancestrally, I am drawn from two waters: First Nations (Alaska Native) and European (German immigrants). My paternal ancestor was first a missionary in Africa and then a pastor of a Lutheran Church in Michigan City, Indiana. I am a direct descendent of the Athabascan people who originally lived on the Lower Tanana (about a hundred miles or so from Fairbanks, Alaska). Our Native name is *Ten Hut'ænæ*, literally "trail people"—my ancestors were hunter-gatherers, and the trail is a part of my spirit as much as anything else. Wherever my trail has led, I take another Athabascan word with me: *nenana*, sometimes translated as a "good place to camp"—my great grandmother is buried in the village by that name. My ancestral name, Yidokodiltona, comes to me in the way all names come: they are given. My ancestors' names, and therefore my own, was taken from us by White missionaries. In this work, I claim back what was ours to begin with. Those who stole it will never return it because they could never keep it. As with my names, I like to think God gives us not only one good place to camp but many such places, and I include the northwest of England, where I have been living since December 2020, as *nenana*. This, too, influences my thoughts about preaching, some of its mystery and some of its ethical responsibilities in a world too familiar with genocide.

There are also literal paths in this book, many of which I have shared with my Lancashire-born wife, Rebecca. The morning she and I left Kirkby Stephen, a small village just east of the Lake District in England, it was overcast but clear. That was down in the valley. Our midday destination was higher up, the Nine Standards Rigg, an ancient assembly of rocks whose purpose history has forgotten. They watch over the valley below Hartley Fell almost like military sentries, as if left by a medieval lord warning strangers to "keep out" of the land beyond the ridge. Walkers come to this site precisely because its origin and purpose are covered in mystery. On the day we visited, it was also enveloped in thick mist. Indeed, our excitement in visiting the Nine Standards slowly dimmed as we continued: mist, blowing in great gasps, made finding our way almost impossible. We could see the path two feet in front of us but not much more. It was classic English weather.

We eventually found the site and, separating, began to explore. I had lost track of Rebecca and she of me when I heard her voice cry out, alarmed: "Rob? Rob? Where are you? Rob?" Where was I? Taking a selfie in front of one of the larger Standards, as I recall. I walked towards her voice and we reunited. "Thank God," she exclaimed. At first, I thought she was relieved to see me, but it turned out her concerns were practical: "I was afraid that you'd left with the maps!"

I hope not to create anxiety by disappearing for a selfie from time to time. I may do that, hopefully in a way that doesn't crowd out your vocation. But there'll be a few teaching moments from my own preaching life. In this mode, I'll be "modeling" the art of preaching—I offer my approach with the understanding that it might not be everyone's cup of tea. Take or leave as you please. I'll also bring maps of the preaching life. I enjoy walking, especially with good company. I also like new trails. I know how to use a compass. Holding on to a few good maps, reading them, equips us for the life of preaching.

Maybe as important as anything I've ever learned is the experience of being lost, knowing that I don't know. And living with it. Or walking with it. Deer hunting in the Sierra Nevada mountains of California, my stepdad said that if I were ever to get lost, don't panic. Up in the mountains, panic kills. If you're lost, they say "stay put"—or in the world of preaching, take a deep breath. Stop for a cup of coffee. Leave the study for a walk around the block. Find different ways of asking for directions, listening rather than acting. Consult the maps of your theological tradition. But don't panic!

Over a lifetime of teaching and preaching, I don't panic too often. That's not quite true. I feel that panic almost every week. It's not something you ever quite shake. But at the same time, I've acquired some wisdom and maybe even a theological clue or two for the journey.

Finding Purpose

Alfred J. Wainwright, the English walker, advises walkers to "always have a definite objective, in a walk as in life—it is so much more satisfying to reach a target by personal effort than to wander aimlessly. An objective in life is an ambition, and life without ambition is . . . well, aimless wandering."[1] A question you might ask yourself, then, is, "What's my ambition in preaching?" Maybe it's too big of a question. I can detect different "ambitions" in

---

1. Wainwright, *Coast to Coast*, vi.

Part One: Callings

my preaching life over the years, some gritty and others teacherly and some I'm not all that proud of (there was, for example, that sermon series based on a bunch of self-help books). Something else to consider: the purity of our ambitions may be counterproductive, especially as they mask the complexities of a lifelong vocation. Wainwright never preached, but he did walk with a practical understanding of the land:

> It is never possible to follow a dead-straight beeline over a long distance without trespassing: climbing fences, wading rivers, perhaps swimming sheets of water, and walking through houses and gardens. In fact, no straight line on a map will give a dead-straight beeline because it is now generally accepted in the best circles that the earth is round, not flat, and a straight line on a map must therefore be incorrect to the extent of the curvature between the two points, however slight.[2]

Wainwright understood the way our "purpose driven" ambitions can mask the complexities and, indeed, riches afforded by a more loving, more generous, patient, and indulgent path.

Limits and boundaries give us gifts. Wainwright's plan for the Coast to Coast (C2C), from which these quotes are taken, suggests that a good walking plan does not only account for the curvature of the earth. As you begin the C2C, you may be thinking about the 190-odd miles of the walk ahead, going from west to east. But from St. Bees, the walker strikes out not to the east, but to the north, walking the slow curve of a coastal path. With the Irish sea to your left, you often look out onto the sea and in the opposite direction of your destination. Those waters, birds circling in the air, the taste of salt, these—and not the far-off destination of Robin Hood's Bay—fix your gaze.

Not until your experience of the path has been thoroughly saturated with the Irish Sea, for four miles or so, do you eventually turn your face eastward, now looking toward the cluster of peaks that make up the Lake District. Did Wainwright plan so that the walker would absorb the place they were preparing to leave, or hope that they would find in the indirection of the footpath an interior direction? He never says. He repeats the pattern again, on the eastern coast, as Wainwright guides his walking companion to their destination, Robin Hood's Bay, a small fishing village on the North Sea of England.

---

2. Wainwright, *Coast to Coast*, vi.

A Peek and It Winks Away

One of the things that makes Wainwright such a delightful companion is that he illustrates, with his own sketches, the peaks and valleys. He wrote his books in the 1950s but drew his sketches so precisely that they are still used by walkers today. But he also records, as if for all of time, moments that would seem to be lost to everyone. Especially memorable for us was a warning he left about a particular farm dog we might meet as we turned east, towards the Lake District. Be ready, he warns, for this dog, which will nip at you if you're not careful. I thought, "That's one thing we don't need to worry about. That dog's long gone by now!" But when we turned east, started through the farm, we were immediately set on by an aggressive farm dog that succeeded in biting Rebecca on the back of her calf. Fortunately, it wasn't a bad bite, but it struck me that part of Wainwright's charm is that while he is accurate, he is also real, sometimes so real that you feel as if you've met the very same dog . . . which of course, couldn't be true . . . could it?

On the very last day of our walk, hewing closely to the path seemed ill-advised. It rained all day. Another couple cut the path, going as straight as possible, by way of the bus. They seemed wise. The path was slick with mud. At one point, we forded a swollen stream after what we took to be the trail tapered out into nothing. By the end, we looked positively wretched.

Do we walk a path? Or does the walk take us on a journey whose end we cannot say and whose moods we cannot predict? For me this is the life of the preacher, or the experience of one who lives with sermons.

On that last day of the C2C it was chucking it down, almost all morning. It was difficult to find the footpath, partly due to the mist and rain but also to the how faint the path had become at that late stage of the journey. It had been clear in the Lake District, but now on the far eastern edge of the Yorkshire Moor, it was difficult to see. Relatively few of those who set out on the walk make it much farther than the Lake District. In the final leg of the C2C, our progress felt slow. Frequent stops to check our map, looking for any sign to orientate, or confirm our way eventually led us to the intersection with the coastal portion of the Cleveland Way. Surprisingly, the weather broke, blue skies revealed themselves, and our pace quickened with anticipation as we walked the final four or five miles to Robin Hood's Bay.

Those who live with the sermon through its times of moody withdrawal, its stroppy behavior, that long-dead dog snarling at our heel, and maybe the sermon's real sicknesses are also witnesses to these times when, almost like a miracle, the sun peeks out from behind clouds of gloom, and we know we're nearly home.

Part One: Callings

I think one of the unique joys in the preacher's life happens somewhere between the first encounter with the text and the sermonic moment of Sunday. If you have experience with sourdough, which many of us acquired during the pandemic, you'll know about a stage in the process where the yeasts kind of go crazy, bubbling, and gassing like a boisterous classroom of kids. It's exciting. But it won't do for the yeast to be overactive if the plan is to make bread with an even rise. What brings order to this creative chaos? Salt, writes one baker. She says salt acts like a teacher coming into a classroom full of kids bubbling over with happy talk. For those who preach, purpose is an especially key ingredient once you've had lots of time to get frothy with the text and its rich possibilities. But beware: as soon as you introduce "purpose" to that batch of creative energy, it will suddenly feel flat, at least for a while.

While it feels flattening, purpose winnows our activities down to something manageable. The root, or *radix* from which we get "radical," of the church's witness is to be found in the untamed spirit of play, even the original Spirit that plays over the face of the inexpressible. Play gives the sermon life to begin with. Without it, there's really no reason to preach. Play suggests for me the woman who poured out the expensive perfume on Jesus' feet. There's a kind of wastefulness in preaching. One of my favorite cartoonists, the writer of Calvin and Hobbes, said that if people saw him in his creative time, they would say he was "goofing off"—some laypeople mistakenly conclude the same about preachers.

Many of us would locate play with the Spirit, or we might use language like "creativity" or "imagination" or "brooding" or the "stewing" phase—it's the phase of the sermonic journey that is not tethered to a particular goal but just breathing the air of possibility. Or tasting that original freedom, where we participate with the freewheeling Path-maker, who leads us and turns us, and teases us with footpaths that we might take one day, and some that we follow without having planned. I'd be willing to wager that, for most sermons, if we can distill just one drop of that spirit for the Lord's Day, it will be like streams of living water.

But distillation . . .

Where I live now, I literally step out the door into one of the most beautiful parts for the world you can imagine: the rolling hills of Lancashire. And it sounds like a cliché but breathing the air, feeling the exertion of the muscles, the landscape rolling away down into Chatburn or Rimington, or farther off to Clitheroe feels intoxicating. From some locations I can see the faint lines of the Irish Sea. At times, the energy of the creation flows, ready at hand, and coming so effortlessly that, when I return to our cottage, I imagine that my fingers will fly over the keyboard . . . and as soon as I sit at my desk, the task narrows to something specific, and the energy and vision that I had felt only moments ago seems to vanish into a mist of particular tasks, which are further thwarted by my limitations as a thinker and wordsmith.

I start looking for a rest stop or for refreshment.

You will want to know about the Lion Inn of this book, the way it peeks at you and then winks away.

"I don't so much write a book," says Annie Dillard, "as sit up with it, as with a dying friend. During visiting hours, I enter its room with dread and sympathy for its many disorders. I hold its hand and hope it will get better."[3] Dillard inspired the title for this book, *Living with the Sermon*. On a Friday night, people sometimes ask their ministers, "Is your sermon done yet?" We answer by estimating our time to completion because to say that we are, at that moment, living with the sermon, would be too much for the congregation to hear. What is it like to live with this thing? Not easy. But there are ways we can make it less difficult. I touch on homiletics because it deals with the science of preaching, and to that extent it often helps with not only diagnosis but treatment. But my real interest is in the person and community that lives with the sermon, and this is more than homiletics or being "finished" with the sermon or not.

Living requires more than a biological rhythm, a body capable of maintaining homeostasis; we find refreshment and perspective at the boundaries. I think of the sermon as folly or weakness, to cite Paul's language (2 Cor. 12:9). Just as people live with pain or with disability, we live with sermons—they also write them, speak them, listen to them, and forget them—but we live with the sermon, or the sermon lives in a feverish state with us. As it finds expression, Christ turns what seems like weakness, and is weakness, into strength. To some extent, this book reflects my experience with that fever and how sometimes, during our homiletical visits, that sickness turns to something good.

---

3. Dillard, *Writing Life*, 52.

Part One: Callings

Organization

The book falls into three parts, Callings, Tinkering, and Community. Part One orients the reader to a human calling of the preacher, particularly using disability thinking to name the way of the cross and resurrection in human journeys. Tinkering in Part Two takes us to the homiletical workshop where, to continue the theme of disability, we learn to use the prosthetic tongue of the preaching moment, as an event of speaking that arises from careful thinking. Part Three, Community, shifts the emphasis from pulpit to pew. How can the sermon be an occasion for intentional human formation as well as reconciliation? When confronted by difficult topics in the preaching life, do we turn back (choose an easier gospel) or, if possible, find a better way for a costly gospel? What do teachers and psychologists teach us about creating a safer space when reflecting on difficult issues? Given the limits of a good speech, how do we foster a safer space for personal learning, processing, and discovering in the life of a congregation?

Throughout expect to see a few "homiletical visits" with our sick sermon as we think about different aspects of sermon construction, delivery, and the dialogical shape of the sermon for the congregation. Each chapter concludes with "Signposts for the Footpath" that may be sermonic, or homiletical (pointers for homiletical travel, nothing fancy, just a helpful recommendation), or perhaps something like a preacher's memoir. Or refreshment, to continue the metaphor of the Lion Inn.

Chapter 2, "Unfit for Preaching," asks, "Why the metaphor of walking for preaching?" While walking may be fitness for some, for people who are poor it is the predominant mode of transportation. For the most part, Jesus walked, apart from a ride on a donkey (or two) and that little walk on the water. In this chapter, we use the lens of disability theory, especially as described in Nancy Eiesland's landmark work *The Disabled God: Toward a Liberation Theology of Disability*: her anthropology suggests a "transformed understanding of independence, premised not on physical detachment but rather on relatedness and solidarity." The God she describes speaks and lives from "outside of able-bodied categories."[4] Probing in a christological direction, Kosuke Koyama sees to the heart of who we proclaim, observing that throughout his life, Jesus walked until in crucifixion Jesus lost his mobility.[5] Perhaps the immobility of cross and cradle are endpoints on the same journey and a warning against ableist approaches to any theological practice, including preaching. I take ambulation as a metaphor for travel and as a freely chosen disability compared to other ways of moving.

Chapter 3, "Haunted like Holy Things," explores the way biblical narrators leave readers signs of God's actions—or more signals of God's presence-absence in and among the verbs of narrative. For those who live with sermons, it may be nothing less than "tracking" the movements of God. And yet, it is also true that God pursues us, indeed this is the first truth. This paradox is at once exegetical and mystical, a highly cognitive exercise and a form of spirituality. Could we say that it speaks to the preacher's peculiar spirituality, haunted by holy things? Exegesis or, literally, bringing out the text does not strike one as an obviously spiritual exercise, but we begin to see that theologically rich exegesis may only be possible as a kind of spiritual practice. Through this chapter, hunter and haunted, we will wander through Luke and to an ICU Trauma Center—in this way we will find clues for the way verbs, as unstable and indeterminate things, tease us in one direction before surprising us in another.

Chapter 4 is "Creature Comforts." There is no question about the importance of parchments for the preaching life (recall Paul's instructions to Timothy—he asks him to "only do not forget to bring the parchments") but sometimes we forget the first part of that text: do *"bring* my cloak" (2 Tim 4:13)! Dietrich Bonhoeffer, while in prison, asked his parents for books . . . and that pair of slacks he's sure he left in the closet or (frequently) for tobacco. Pastors are fed by frequent and regular interactions with the parchments of our theological tradition, and we rely on little helps along the way. Yes, we will remember the parchments, but let's not forget the cloak of help we will need when we're stuck between a funeral, a grumpy church secretary (they're always grumpy), and a leaky pipe in the basement—in other words, bring my cloak, please. I've dubbed the familiar way preachers connect Scripture to world and world to Scripture as a kind of "creature comfort" that preachers depend on in the week to week. It is not the "original" thought, but the tradition of wisdom that we transplant into

---

4. Eiesland, *Disabled God*, 38.
5. Koyama, *Three Mile an Hour God*, 7.

Part One: Callings

new mediums, as we map Christian patterns onto the world and worldly patterns onto Christ.

Chapter 5 is entitled "Wooden Tongue." Maybe to the congregation on Sunday it seems as if the sermon blossomed from the pulpit that very morning—but those who live with sermons know that this is only partially true. We will want to think in the minutest detail about our work. In different parlance, we're talking about the written word as a prosthetic for the spoken. Is the manuscript the enemy of the tongue? Yes, in some ways it is. But it can also be a powerful tool, an extension for an absence (and hence the metaphor of the prosthetic tongue) and even something capable of bringing beauty. Closely related to this topic is the role of the self-edit. How do we improve our skill as preachers? What I want to help with is the formation of the art of the edit—this includes thinking about the fits and starts of the writing life, the way we revisit those efforts, and a glimpse of how a beginning becomes a beginning (sneak peek—it isn't usually what you wrote in your first draft). So, we'll be about the art of the life of composing and tactical or tactile recompositions of your work.

Chapter 6 considers "Coloring by Numbers." This chapter works out three basic ways of mapping the sermon: through basic qualities of the sermon (unity, balance, variety, and dynamism); literary forms in the Bible; the analogical pattern of interpretation; and more abstract forms of sermon organization. As the chapter title suggests, I'm trying to think about the form of the sermon as something that we can talk about in an abstract way but, when we learn to use it, it can talk back to us. This is the way a formalist poet describes his experience of poetic forms—they think back at him. Talking about sermon form as "coloring by numbers" is a tongue-in-cheek way of saying there is something more to sermonic form than meets the eye—knowing a form or two is a convenience but it is also a meaningful parameter that creates a different kind of thought than the one you might if you had no external rule at all.

Chapter 7, "Wee Gaggles," asks us to think about ways in which we can return the sermon to the congregation. Our journey with God can be deep and sustained, rather than just a series of pit stops on Sunday, which are memorable in some way . . . or maybe not. Pastors pour probably half their workweek into the sermon and even more of their heart and thinking—and then at the narthex, we talk about the weather, or, "How 'bout those Cubs?" A friend of mine suggested that I start a Wee Gaggle after the sermon, a sermon-related group talk of about fifteen or twenty minutes.

These were popular. I'm convinced that our congregations want to digest the sermon but the patterns of worship—come, get, and leave—don't always accommodate that exercise. Your congregation grows through not only "hearing" and "obeying" but testing the sermonic ideas against their experience of life—and you will grow as a pastoral theologian as you hear God's people reflecting on biblical texts, theological ideas, claims you've made in the sermon, and experiences of life. This chapter offers some suggestions to help us achieve a greater level of congregational ownership of the sermon.

Chapter 8 regards "Difficult Journeys." In this chapter we take on the question of preaching in a context of high trauma and strong denial, particularly around the issue of White people and whiteness. These are treacherous homiletical waters. Preaching has always been dangerous but now, against the rise of White Christian nationalism, the call to name the sickness of whiteness feels not so much like a "sermon to get up for Sunday" but a call to combat a particular kind of disease, beginning with the way that disease manifests itself in White people. This chapter reflects on how, broadly, we introduce difficult topics to a Sunday morning church (trigger warnings) as well as how, beyond the sermon, we foster learning in any context that is otherwise often (and understandably) antagonistic. While it is debatable whether a sermon can teach people how to be anti-racist, it is possible that people can learn what that means, in a human way, through creative exercises that offer participants a safer place for a dangerous topic.

Chapter 9 focuses on "Distance Walking." Many of us learned the sermon as a sprint—where we learned this is difficult to say, but there are the usual suspects: procrastination, happy success of the successful sermon we wrote in fifteen minutes, or it was born of necessity (too many crises in the pastoral week). Whatever its origin, for good reasons and maybe some not so good, the sprint mentality of sermon preparation may become dominant for us. This is not a recipe for longevity in ministry or richness in preaching. We can't sprint vocation. In this chapter, we explore ways in which we can increase our consciousness of the whole of the preaching life as well as a kind of breadth of vision for our lives as those who preach. We'll talk about reading plans and strategies, including some thoughts about how we can get more distance from the Revised Common Lectionary (or another reading plan); the value of a coach or pastor supervisor who can help us reflect on our work; and giving ourselves permission to preach the "good enough" sermon, mindful that imperfection may also be a form of testimony to the Spirit who speaks not through our strength but through our weakness.

Part One: Callings

Walking Preacher of the Burden

The journal *Image* published a series of pencil drawings by Jack Baumgartner. His work explores themes of pilgrimage, especially a series entitled *The Legend of Walking Man*. In this drawing, Baumgartner evokes the journey of spirituality through the adventures of a person who appears to be on a pilgrimage through mostly barren landscapes with only a blackbird for companionship. "Walking Man of the Burden" carries a backpack that bristles with discomfort.[6] And the pack seems self-important, as if you can't drop this, change it, much less adapt it. It suggests something like Christendom; or the explicit tension between person and tradition; or your theological education writ large. You ask, "Was the pack made for the sojourner or the sojourner for the pack?" The pack seems important, but how? One clue might be in what Walking Man *chooses* as creature comfort for the journey. A walking stick. A pair of boots. A belt. How many times has that walking stick saved him? Or been a companion? Is it worn smooth with his grip? What about the boots? Or the leather of the belt, with its familiar bend and wear, does it tell a story, too? What things give this pilgrim comfort, not only because they are useful but because they are shaped with habit? Our wanderer looks away from the viewer, toward an indistinct horizon, almost as if he's trying to turn but finds it difficult. A blackbird, perhaps a raven, haunts the sky to his right, as if calling the pilgrim in another direction—and perhaps suggesting a something other than the burden on the pilgrim's back.

We will return to the mysterious blackbird . . . but first the backpack. What does it represent for you? When we think about the peculiar backpack of *Walking Preacher*, maybe we think of denominational systems, or medieval theological disputes dropped into twenty-first–century contexts, or impossibly complex paths of interpretive traditions, not to mention the life of the congregational leader, which seems to be needled with anxiety and distraction. Or perhaps we think of the unique burdens that are placed on those who preach: who else crafts a formal speech each week, is reliably witty, insightful, informed, easily speaks to multiple generations, is timely, includes memorable quips and stories, speaks just the right word during crisis, and does so as a scholar, and with virtually no help, apart from the church secretary whose main concern is getting the worship information together before Sunday?

---

6. Reprinted by permission of the artist.

Part One: Callings

It reminds me of this sketch. Has preaching always been such a burden? It was not always so, at least not for me. One of the first sermons I preached, for the congregation that baptized me (I was a college student at the time) had as its inspiration the cover of a book that I'd found at the university library showing the sleek body of the famous clipper ship charging through the wild oceans, masts full of wind. I hadn't read much more than the blurb on the back cover. I think I probably read John 3:8: "The wind blows where it chooses, and you hear the sound of it, but you do not know where it comes from or where it goes."

I consulted around about zero commentaries. I was twenty years old. What more did I need? As I recall, it was a good sermon.

Today, I can't imagine stepping into a congregation on Sunday morning with a book cover as inspiration. I never told my students (or anyone else for that matter) about that sermon—but there it is. I don't commend that as a model of preaching, and yet I feel wistful for that freedom. Bob Jacks, professor at Princeton Seminary, said something like that in one of his classes, as he fervently hoped that students would surrender their voices to the movement of the Spirit, let their winged words find some lofty perch. Instead, too often, he felt as if his students were lost in densely written commentaries or other academic jargon.

It is not only students. Instead of flying on the wings of the Spirit, many of us feel tethered to the obligations of our theological education—the *rights and responsibilities* of that education. Sometimes the combined weight of "scholarship" and "originality" and the disease of "attributive mania" (a pathology common among academics) is enough to break the back of today's preacher. Is it possible to carry the burden of contemporary notions of originality, heavy tomes of biblical commentary and theological systems, and footnotes for every gulp of air—and, oh yes, don't forget the vision of the Spirit—into the pulpit without feeling the joy of the preaching life turn into the whimpering protests of aching joints and sore backs?

What art or form of intellectual life feels right for those who live with the sermon? Is it only one kind of life? Is it a theological purebred or is it a mix of things? How does it come to take its shape? Was it something we found in a box crammed with spare screws, wires, an out of place fishing fly, a fragment of something someone said, a sheared off piece that you found while running your fingers through the accumulated junk and you said, "Voila! this is just the thing"?

A Peek and It Winks Away

We will think about the burden that we carry with us, how we carry it and why, to reconceptualize things to fit our path so that we do not quite lose sight of the raven that haunts our way—how do we hold light or perhaps how do we release it from the containers of creaturely control?

The black bird in the Baumgartner drawing reminds me of the creation myth of Raven, well-known among Native people in the Pacific Northwest. The myth of Raven recounts how, before time began, this mercurial character, Raven, stole light from a box kept by a greedy chief and flung it into the world. That light gave shape and space to everything in the world, according to the legend. A shape-shifter, never quite resolved into a fixed thing, the Raven injects something unpredictable, a being that is clever or devious or both, into the myth of creation. Raven toggles between multiple personalities, bipolar divisions, sometimes disguised as a spruce needle, sometimes as disreputable thief who steals light, and sometimes a generous liberator, black as night, who gives light.

Maybe the raven acts as a symbol of the preacher's muse, its burden light and its mystery a darkness sometimes visible.

Chapter Two

Unfit for Preaching

"You'll be crippled!"

—My stepdad when I told him I was walking the Camino de Santiago.

In 1999, I traveled to Europe, initially Paris, for the summer. Ostensibly, I was in Europe for language study, but the real reason was to walk the Camino de Santiago, a five-hundred-mile medieval pilgrimage, popularized by Emilio Estevez's film *The Way* (2010). The night before I left Paris to begin the walk, I called my parents back home in the States and announced that, the next day, I would be taking the train to the small village of St. Jean Pied de Port, one of the traditional starting points of the Camino. "You'll be crippled!" was my stepdad's reaction. I was instantly deflated. Those were not words that I wanted to hear at that moment, in part because there was enough truth to them that I had to weigh them carefully. At a more basic level, I had to ask myself, "Why am I doing this?" It didn't "fit" into whatever norm I had conceived for myself.

I did not sleep well that night. But I did eventually walk (and, towards the end, limped) some five-hundred miles. This is not a book about that pilgrimage, but a related one: the preaching life as pilgrimage. That's not an original way of thinking about preaching, preaching as journey, or the preacher as pilgrim or the sermonic path.

So why, you ask, another book looking at preaching through the lens of peripatetic activity? Maybe because my stepdad's reaction contains a kernel of truth. Crippled. That word, cruel as it feels, recalls for me the area of disability studies. I am not equipped to capture the full range and complexity of the field. Nevertheless, without becoming a disability theorist or trying to represent this work as a "homiletic of disability," this field of inquiry helps me think through the preaching vocation and maybe it also sheds light on my experiences as an educator, preacher, and human being.

Walking with Unrest

Abraham Lincoln preferred preachers who appeared as if they were being attacked by a great hive of bees over those who spoke with fluid eloquence. Lincoln, tortured as he was by depression, knew what he was listening for.

As a professor who often supported the admissions team of the seminary, I read student applications. In their admissions file, you would see the usual suspects: degrees earned, work experience, scores on standard exams and grade point averages, a faculty interview. But if you were like me, you flipped to the essay portion of the application, often entitled "Journey of Faith"—or something close. In this section, students told their stories. Over the years, I began to discern a pattern to these stories. It was often narrated as something overcome, a setback that was eclipsed by progress in the journey of faith. That was to be expected, given that candidates wanted to make the best representation of themselves to seminary admissions.

As much as I wanted to believe in these stories of heroic success, the things they shared were not trivial. It might be an unexpected death, a divorce, the onset of disease, a professional/life crisis, or perhaps national crisis. Today, the crisis named by some is creational. I began to wonder whether these were not mischaracterized as obstacles overcome. Perhaps these were the irritants or the unresolved questions that triggered the decision for seminary and a life of interpretation.

Why were these struggles being suppressed in their admissions narratives? I'm not suggesting they were being dishonest—or that the admissions process was dishonest. But was this dance between applicant and admissions an ableist theology masquerading as Christ's body? What happens when the mask comes off? Not all preachers grapple with such issues, and many who do learn to live with them and flourish, but I often wonder if the bifurcated way organizations treat the "products" of students (and especially preachers) over and against the people they are contributes to the harm.

Do we understand ourselves?

Do people respond to the call to preach because they claim abilities or because they are captive to a call, a perhaps crippling vocation?

It Is Solved in Walking

People joined the Camino de Santiago for different reasons. A same-sex couple walked together, one supporting his partner in the face of growing sickness. Another confided that he was torn up with guilt over his wife's declining health and his infidelity. Some, of course, walked because it was a personal challenge or purely for fitness or viewed it as a religiously themed holiday. Most walked with some form of unrest on the inside and their companions alongside—and maybe all of us joined the path because it is solved in walking.

Echoes of crisis and wholeness connect those who undertake pilgrimage and those who make the pew-to-pulpit journey. It may be a few short steps from the pew to the pulpit, but the journey entails the question or the mystery of being human that may never be fully answered because it takes more than a lifetime to answer it. Perhaps that's the purpose of this chapter—to get us into the intersecting roots of each life, into our mutual callings, where broken hearts become one together.

To the writers of Scripture, experiences of limited function form an important part of God's calling. Was Isaac, for instance, born with a learning disability? The narrator of Genesis portrays Isaac as visibly compliant. Opposite Isaac's seeming passivity, we see Abraham's methodical actions: "bound" and "laid" him on top of the wood (22:9b). Later in life, the narrator reports that Isaac's eyes had grown "dim" while the machinations of Rebekah and Jacob grew sharp with the goal of purloining Isaac's blessing from Esau (27:1–17). Isaac's stark vulnerability plays out again in the act of Jacob's impersonation of Esau (27:18–29). When Isaac belatedly discovers the scheme, the narrator says that "he trembled violently" (27:33).

Perhaps the blessing of Isaac foreshadowed something other than the privilege Jacob sought. That's one possible meaning of the injury he acquires while wrestling with the stranger in 32:22–31: "When the man saw that he did not prevail against Jacob, he struck him on the hip socket; and

Unfit for Preaching

Jacob's hip was put out of join as he wrestled with him" (32:25). He walks on, passing Penuel, "limping because of his hip" (32:31). Just as he had deceived his father, Jacob's sons will also deceive him with the fabricated story (the hairy fabric an echo of Esau's hairy arm?) of Joseph's death by a wild animal (37:29–35).

Moses provides another clue. He responds to Yahweh's call by listing objections to this invitation: Who am I that I should go to Pharaoh? (Exodus 3:11); I don't really know who you are so how I can I go? (3:13); what if they don't believe that you sent me? (4:1); and, finally, as his capstone objection, Moses lists a speech impediment: "O my Lord, I have never been eloquent, neither in the past nor even now that you have spoken to your servant; but I am slow of speech and slow of tongue" (4:10). In vss. 11–12, the Lord appears to completely dismiss Moses' objection and then, in the next moment, proposes the mouth of the Lord as the divine "prosthetic" for Moses' malfunctioning tongue: "Who gives speech to mortals? Who makes them mute or deaf, seeing or blind? Is it not I, the Lord? Now go, I will be with your mouth and teach you what you are to speak." That might have ended all argument, except Moses pleads again: "Please send someone else" (4:13)—as in, send for another body altogether! The Lord continues to bargain with Moses: "What of your brother Aaron the Levite? I know that he can speak fluently" (4:14). Just as the Lord is the "mouth" of Moses' prophetic speech, so Aaron will be the "tongue" for Moses' glossal stump.

Ezekiel's calling portrays the prophet as one suffering from the post-traumatic stress experienced by violent exile and displacement: "The spirit lifted me up and bore me away; I went in bitterness in the heat of my spirit, the hand of the Lord being strong upon me. I came to the exiles at Tel-abib, who lived by the river Chebar. And I sat there among them, stunned, for seven days" (Ezek 3:14–15). Isaiah seems more receptive of the calling of God than either Ezekiel or Jeremiah, but the message he is assigned to deliver seems the opposite of liberative but proactively disabling: "Go and say to this people: Keep listening but do not comprehend, keep looking but do not understand. . . . Stop their ears, shut their eyes so that they may not look with their eyes and listen with their ears and comprehend with their minds and turn and be healed" (Isa 6:9–10).

Each narrative of calling includes an expression of a diminishment or loss of function that continues as a visible mark in the life of the called: a lifelong stutter, a limp, or lingering symptoms of trauma. Are these in some way a window onto peculiar forms of imagination? Or is the core vocation of speaking in God's name evoked by Isaiah: "The holy seed is its stump" (Isa 6:13)? Is the seed of human testimony to be found in the glossal stump?

The story of Naomi in the book of Ruth ends with a tantalizing image of the interdependency of the body in solidarity, the stump of maternity as a seed for a renewed eschatological imagination. Naomi, beyond her childbearing years (1:11), becomes a mother who nurses Ruth's son, Obed: "Then Naomi took the child and laid him in her bosom, and became his nurse. The women of the neighborhood gave him a name, saying, 'A son has been born to Naomi'" (4:16–17). The narrator makes no attempt to "smooth" out the asymmetry and incongruities of Naomi's condition with this radically new constellation of human relationships. The narrator presents us with the new creation.

In the Acts account, the Spirit of Christ assaults Paul, leaving him visually impaired: "Though his eyes were open, he could see nothing; so they led him by the hand" (9:8). In Acts 26:9, Paul complains of political captivity ("'except for these chains'") and in his letters speaks of a "physical thorn" that was not removed. God's power, he comes to believe, is made perfect in weaknesses, where Christ dwells powerfully (2 Cor 12:7–10). He will offer as his signature the "stigmata" on his body, the wounds that testify to a more lasting wholeness than physical health alone (Gal 6:17).

Culture teaches us to think of disability as a temporary loss of function. What if function is the anomaly and not the other way around? Culture teaches us that disability is something to be overcome with heroic and often individualistic efforts being rewarded. By implication, those who live with disabilities are somehow less human. Could we be more human when we live ordinary lives with unique challenges? Without valorizing disability as somehow essential, the recurring theme of these biblical accounts suggests that loss of function is far more common and far more ordinary than we would like to imagine. Could it also be that in the economy of salvation, loss of function serves as a kind of marker in calling, a sign, like the limp of Jacob? Or the emptiness of Naomi?

Here Was God for Me

Nancy Eiesland's landmark work *The Disabled God: Toward a Liberation Theology of Disability* describes what she calls a personal epiphany, one that she did not expect:

> ... I had waited for a mighty revelation of God. But my epiphany bore little resemblance to the God I was expecting or the God of my dreams. I saw God in a sip-puff wheelchair, that is, the chair used by most quadriplegics enabling them to maneuver by blowing and sucking on a strawlike device. Not an omnipotent, self-sufficient God, but neither a pitiable, suffering servant. In this moment, I beheld God as a survivor, unpitying and forthright. I recognized the incarnate Christ in the image of those judged "not feasible," "unemployable," with "questionable quality of life." Here was God for me.[1]

That image suggests a beginning point for me, a dramatic reformation of our christological imagination with implications for our anthropology.

Disability studies underline experiences of liminality, being suspended between two worlds or seeing the world with two sets of eyes. Whether through pilgrimage as volitional act or forced migration, we come to think about the "liminal" path of being between worlds. We walk in risky space. "For Jesus, leaving home, as it would be for anyone in his circumstances, was an act of grave consequences," writes Sang Hyun Lee. "Leaving home meant going out of the structure of one's life. It meant entering a wilderness, a liminal place."[2] Lee's insight echoes Wendell Berry's thoughts on the way a human being enters the wilderness:

> In comparison to the usual traveler with his dependence on machines and highways and restaurants and motels—on the economy and government, in short—the man who walks into the wilderness is naked indeed. He leaves behind his work, his household, his duties, his comforts—even, if he comes alone, his words. He immerses himself in what he is not. It is a kind of death.[3]

People who live with disabilities report that they "leave home" daily as they enter a wilderness where the "temporarily able-bodied" (a term used among disability activists) build a society that amplifies and codifies forms of dependency, paternalism, and exclusion.

According to Eiesland a theology of disability compels an exodus out of the illusion of independence in the majority culture by reactivating symbols in which there are "hidden histories" of human lives that have been suppressed. Reconstituting the symbol of resurrection through the

1. Eiesland, *Disabled God*, 89.
2. Lee, *From a Liminal Place*, 64.
3. Berry, *Unforeseen Wilderness*, 57.

lens of disability, she activates Jesus' resurrection appearance in Luke 24:39: "'Look at my hands and my feet; see it is I myself. Touch me and see; for a ghost does not have flesh and bones as you see that I have.'" Eiesland recasts (or recovers) Jesus' limbs as "impaired hands and feet."[4] Jesus rejects able-bodied projections as false imagining ("I am not a ghost")—those marks are our marks; those impairments our impairments; that life our life. She concludes: "The disabled God is not only the One from heaven but the revelation of true personhood, underscoring the reality that full personhood is fully compatible with the experience of disability."[5]

Real Church and the Fragility of Life

Dietrich Bonhoeffer's thoughts about disability speak to a christological stance that moves us from the idols of success and health to a Lord who lives, quite plainly, within the ordinary limits of the human condition. In so doing, Bonhoeffer builds a case for theological realism in the church. Realism comes by doing theology with a "view from below"—or *in Christ* with a view from below. Realism, or real life and the real church, exist because Jesus Christ enters the world as the Real Human Being.

Incarnation does not underwrite human ideals or speak so much of a heaven out there, but instead of a God who through Christ enters fully, and more fully than we can imagine or experience, into the suffering of the human condition. Bonhoeffer disputes the notion that the disabled need the help of the temporarily able bodied to be human. Rather, he argues the opposite: it is those who know the fragility of life who must be revered and listened to.

Bonhoeffer's experience was shaped by a visit to Bethel near Bielefeld. Bethel's sole purpose was to care for the weak and fragile. He reports what feels like an epiphany, an epiphany with a view from below. He wrote to his grandmother in August 1933:

> I have just come back from the worship service. It is an extraordinary sight, the whole church filled with crowds of epileptics and other ill persons, interspersed with the deaconesses and deacons who are there to help in case one of them fall; then there are the elderly tramps who come in off the country roads, the theological

---

4. Eiesland, *Disabled God*, 100.
5. Eiesland, *Disabled God*, 100.

Unfit for Preaching

students, the children from the lab school, doctors, and they are keen listeners and participants.[6]

The temptation might be to minimize this community as a "limited" or unique species of the church, or an idyllic exception. For Bonhoeffer it isn't a limited representation or a unique species of mission. Instead, the Bethel manifested "the real and material form of Christ's existence in the world."

> [The epileptics'] experience of life must be most extraordinary, not having control over their bodies, having to be resigned to the possibility of an attack at any moment. Today in church was the first time this really struck me, as I became aware of these moments. Their situation of being truly defenseless perhaps gives these people a much clearer insight into certain realities of human existence, the fact that we are indeed basically defenseless, than can be possible for healthy persons.[7]

This phenomenon afforded Bonhoeffer with a glimpse of the real church, the real church interrupting ideals of healthy community with a real human existence in community.

Eiesland relates the fascinating story of Diane DeVries. She was born in rural Texas in 1950 without lower limbs and above-elbow upper extremity stumps. She accepts herself as "ordinary though distinct"[8]; she uses some prosthetics, referring to her wheelchair as "my legs," and rejects other prosthetics as alien and obstructive.[9] Most intriguingly, she forms a social image of "unique relations because of her disability."[10] She self-describes as a person who dances and runs, which seems improbable. Eiesland attributes this to her "active imagination" and to DeVries's relationship to her able-bodied sister. DeVries's explanation is particularly interesting:

> It's true that there is a Diane within this Diane who can dance which enabled me to teach my younger sister Debbie, but there's another reason I could coach her so well. It's hard to explain. Ever since Deb could walk she was taking care of me. I saw her body move from childhood's awkwardness to adult gracefulness and strength. But not only did I see this, I felt her movements. In a sense, part of her body was mine too. So, since I knew how her

---

6. Bonhoeffer, "Letter to Julie Bonhoeffer, August 20, 1933," 370.
7. Bonhoeffer, "Letter to Julie Bonhoeffer, August 20, 1933," 370.
8. Eiesland, *Disabled God*, 35.
9. Eiesland, *Disabled God*, 37–38.
10. Eiesland, *Disabled God*, 38.

body moved, I could coach her in dancing. *Do you understand any of this?*[11]

Eiesland observes the way Diane "shapes new categories of embodiment and normality that include her perception of her sister's body as a resource for constructing her own body image." Her body image suggests a "transformed understanding of independence, premised not on physical detachment but rather on relatedness and solidarity." She also knows that her experience exists "outside of able-bodied categories."[12]

DeVries's account of her participation in her sister's body points to the idea of how preachers may participate, respectfully and with humility, in experience which is best grasped with Bonhoeffer's "view from below." Or perhaps as we eavesdrop on the experience of another. We begin to feel human to the extent that our being human is expressed in the thickness of a sociality of relations—those who live with the fragility of bodies remind us of the truth in all bodies.

Our Relationship to Sickness

The mask that institutional Christianity declares as healthy is often only the myth of the successful or strong. Jesus enters our weakness. The rich person who gives up his wealth begins to feel the shame and fear of poverty. This is suffering. The miracle of Christianity, according to Simone Weil, is not that Christianity makes suffering go away but that it makes it useful.[13] That certainly rings true for many of us who have lived with some form of marginalization. We don't enjoy the marginalization that comes from clinical depression or PTSD or a physical disability or from being a minority. But for those who have experienced the saving health of Jesus, it rings true that this suffering is not without meaning. Christ enters and inhabits weakness; Christ turns our weakness into power—part of Christ's body is ours too. I am not a ghost, but I am made of flesh and bones like you.

Health or wholeness does not come by avoiding sickness but only through a different kind of attunement to sickness.

---

11. Eiesland, *Disabled God*, 38 (italics mine).
12. Eiesland, *Disabled God*, 38.
13. Weil, *Gravity and Grace*, 73.

Unfit for Preaching

Why do the Gospels report that Jesus healed the sick? Or that he touched those afflicted with disease? Why does Jesus seem drawn to life situations that otherwise "normal" people flee or ignore?

Jesus cares for people. Jesus also connects with people, perhaps the people who are most obviously unwell, but also those who live as spectators, thinking that life never touches them, that suffering is either contagious or that their relative health is some verdict about their intrinsic worth, goodness, or divine favor. In the preaching moment, are we also trying to connect to the untouchable parts of human life?

I think so.

The Psalms speak in so many ways about the human condition—some believe that the psalmists give expression to virtually every human experience. Bonhoeffer reminds us that even though these are human words, and human experiences, they are God's words, and God's experiences. Praying the Psalms is, in a way, learning to breathe with God. Bonhoeffer would say that to pray the Psalms is to pray with the prayers of Christ. The psalmist gives us a pattern, bookending the Psalms with the healthy soul who praises God, rejoices in God, joins the creation in endless doxology. Yet throughout the Psalms, you find other less wholesome voices—anger, depression, social anxiety, shame, loneliness, paranoia, fear, confusion, and others.[14]

After confiding to a friend that I struggled with depression, I mentioned that I had begun praying the Psalms. Alarmed, she suggested that perhaps I ought *not* pray the Psalms: "Read something more cheerful," she advised. "I worry about you reading the Psalms, they can be so dark!" She knew the psalmist . . . and there is a kind of danger in the psalmist's laments, in the writer's way of lashing out against "enemies"—if you don't feel the least bit queasy when the psalmist relishes the taste of his enemy's blood, I worry for you . . . and your neighbor. Walter Brueggemann speaks of Psalm 88, the loneliest of all the psalms, as "an embarrassment to conventional faith."[15] It ends at verse 18 without either hope or answer: "You have caused friend and neighbor to shun me; my companions are in darkness." The absence of an "answer" to the psalmist's complaint is telling—and intentional. Platitudes will not remedy its disease. It speaks its truth and waits. Brueggemann asks, "[W]hat is a psalm like that doing in our Bible?"[16] He offers two reasons for its inclusion. First, life is that way: "These poems intend to

---

14. See Bonhoeffer, *Prayerbook of the Bible*.
15. Brueggemann, *Message of the Psalms*, 78.
16. Brueggemann, *Message of the Psalms*, 80.

speak to all of life, not just the good parts. Here, more than anywhere else, faith faces life as it is."[17] Second, it speaks, gives voice rather than being resigned in mute depression. It grows out of Israel's identity: Israel must deal with Yahweh in his life-giving strength and answer. "Israel must also deal with Yahweh in silence, in God's blank absence . . . to be Israel [and to be fully human] means to address God, even in God's unresponsive absence."[18] It ends without hope. Or rather, perhaps it would be best to say that Psalm 88's note sounds almost like defiance in a book where the theological compass mostly points north to happiness.

Proximal Relationships

Mostly, when we think of the walk or the footpath, we think of beautiful landscapes. I'm not going to deny that those pastoral images speak to me and they always will. But I continue to be intrigued by an experience I had on the Camino de Santiago. The pilgrim passes through the hearts of major cities. At times, on that road, you sojourn with people who are not temporarily on the road, but for whom the road is life, the road is home. I vividly remember visiting with people who were unhoused. I did not know they were not on the "official" path. Either housed or unhoused, we looked alike: road weary. The difference between us almost vanished.

The idea of proximity is about how we occupy space or with whom.

What happens, for instance, when the footpath of the sermon takes us to the Federal Building of Baltimore where we stand in solidarity with a family facing deportation? In broken English, a woman, currently living in a sanctuary church because she is undocumented, pleads for her husband who is being held inside the bureaucratic colossus behind us. Her oldest son, a teenager with a learning disability, stands beside her. Your children play with her two younger children, jumping from the concrete walls, running up and down the stairs of the Federal Building. They saw their father disappear into that building. Will he come out? Or will he disappear into a system of deportation?

Or how does your witness change when you join a Border Patrol agent, listening to him tell his story, as he drives you around Douglas, Arizona, just north of the US/Mexico border. He tells you he is divorced. Working with Border Patrol wasn't his first choice for a career in law enforcement.

17. Brueggemann, *Message of the Psalms*, 80.
18. Brueggemann, *Message of the Psalms*, 81.

Unfit for Preaching

He tells you that when he finally catches an "illegal" he asks them, in Spanish, "How is it in your village?" He tells you he always brings them water, feeds them when they are in his custody. Every day, he tells you, before he jumps in his patrol vehicle, he puts on the full armor of Christ, helmet, shield, sidearm, and a police baton "to break the ankle" of a fleeing human being. As you sit in his passenger seat, does it make it easier to preach or does that experience cause the "sermon" to withdraw from an easy clarity?

What happens to the person who preaches, the person who is formed in you as you stand outside a city jail with a Catholic layperson and "Shortie"? They invited you along to show hospitality to those being released from Baltimore's City Jail. Proclaiming release to the captives includes you passing out cigarettes or showing them over to Shortie's barbecue trailer. On the back of the trailer, Shortie has stenciled in his tagline: "Barbecue so good it's illegal." You imagined you knew something about "setting the captives free" but here it means letting the released captives use your phone so they can get a lift or let their family know they're free or simply in a different kind of prison. For Shortie, it's about salvaging dignity. Almost all these men, he says, live with shame—no one knows they're here. It dawns on you this is the opposite of graduation. The young people, almost all young Black men, walk into a world devoid of encouragement and laden with shame.

Who are you now? Who are you here? Shortie asks if you know the story of Job. Yes, you say. "No," he snaps, "you don't. Have you ever been in prison?" he asks. No. "What you know," he says, "you learned in a book." Job isn't a story for Shortie. This place, just outside the Baltimore City Jail, manifests the reality of a church that appears only in action and testimony. It includes real human beings, material solidarity, and frictions. You don't know Job without the suffering . . . or freedom without the captive.

Or as one rapper sings, "The only way to found is lost."

What happens when you go to the trauma center, where you know a seven-year-old gunshot victim is struggling for her life, a few floors away? Can you help her? Can she help herself? Where is the God who helps?

These places are often unnamed or avoided. Yet they have the power to become the space where we imagine the gospel . . . we will have to pray for a long time to hear the sermon from the person who dwells in these places.

Part One: Callings

Signposts for the Footpath

A charge to the University of Dubuque Theological Seminary graduating class of 2015.[19]

Today is a day of completion. Of degrees earned. Of privileges and responsibilities accrued. Of strengths confirmed. And yet for your charge, rather than reaffirming your significant achievement, I am moved instead to share with you two modern-day parables, not about strength, but rather of strength won out of weakness, of wisdom out of folly, and hope out of despair.

"I am his hands; he is my eyes," says Jia Haixia of his friend, Jia Wenqi. Together they suggest the first modern-day parable, these two men from a small village in northeastern China: two disabled men, one blind, the other a double amputee. They work together.

"We are good partners," they say of one another. Their work? Planting a forest.[20] One imagines, perhaps, something less ambitious for two disabled men, something with a faster payoff—they get a small income from the local government for their work—even so, perhaps we think they might labor at something more modest, something less likely to be compared to charging windmills.

Their neighbors in the village thought they were crazy. The riverbanks had been barren for years. The villagers were resigned to the river's annual floods, its destruction simply an inescapable part of nature: "Why bother?" they asked. And yet, Wenqi, a double-arm amputee, and Haixia, his blind friend, bothered. Indeed, every day for the past thirteen years, they bothered, taking the same path to work, to plant a forest sapling by sapling, to practice a routine as repetitive as prayer, and perhaps nearly as deep.

See if you can imagine them walking to work together: Wenqi, double-arm amputee, leading the way, sometimes guiding Haixia, his blind friend, who holds Wenqi's empty sleeve as they walk, sometimes carrying Haixia on his back as they cross a river. Or imagine Wenqi's eyes guiding the hands of Haixia as he climbs a tree to harvest cuttings for new plants. Imagine scenes like this, repeated every day for thirteen years.

19. Hoch, "Yet You Shall Be Different."
20. Hawkins, "Two Disabled Men."

Unfit for Preaching

They estimate they have planted ten thousand healthy trees and, of these, three thousand have died. The work isn't fast and neither is the pay. But then again, today, you see forest where once there was only barren land.

"When we work together," they say, "two become one."

Maybe even more than that happens: The village that once laughed at them now helps them fix their tools, water trees, trim weeds. They have even bought saplings to plant.

So often, we imagine our strengths will complete us, bring us wholeness. But what if the parable is right? What if God gives us weakness in order that we might find a better strength, the sacrament of mutual interdependence, a form of interdependence that makes broken people into whole people, and broken societies into reconciling and healing societies?

What if the parable is true?

It goes to other things as well, such as mental illness. Chris Hoke, a street minister in Seattle, believes "all of us [have] a fragile nerve inside of us, like a spiritual antenna deep within our core. Some people," he writes, "simply have . . . abnormally large antennas inside—poets, prophets, psychopaths, your slightly crazy aunt." Maybe even a few preachers, present company excused, of course!

In his work with people in jail, or homeless street kids of downtown Seattle, he has met a lot of young people with schizophrenia:

> I've wondered when talking with them about the abuse and the trauma they've survived, if some wounded people's antenna-nerves are damaged. Maybe they are exposed, jutting out like a bone from a broken arm, picking up way too many of the otherwise faint spiritual frequencies coursing through this world—from beyond, as well as from the person across the room. I've wondered if some of these people slam heroin or meth . . . as a way of jamming cotton into their ears.[21]

The problem, he says, is not that they cannot hear, but that they hear too much.

It's an ancient idea that, in some way, the troubled are indeed connected to the spirit world in a way that "normally" functioning people are not. Like the prophets, who also heard too much, they cry out, as often afflicted by the acuity of their "spiritual antenna" as they are comforted. Maybe that's why Chris shows genuine interest in the voices that the schizophrenic

---

21. Hoke, *Wanted*, 191.

hears. What if what they hear is more than illusion? After all, he says, Galileo thought comets were an illusion.

Perhaps we too imagine knowledge at the expense of wisdom. Indeed, he wonders whether folks like you and I hear too little, not nearly enough. It's almost as if we've suffered an amputation or that our antennas have been badly bent, damaged. And so, he goes to the schizophrenic to hear what he *cannot* hear, to listen to the stories of people who, in the etymology of the word, are torn in two, one side in this world and the other side suspended in another, haunted, often terrifying world. According to Chris, most of the voices they hear are cruel. But there are other times, he says, when another voice seems to break through the crackling static of schizophrenia, a voice that tells them, "You're okay. You belong to me. And I love you." He writes that, through these friendships, he is learning to pray: "I've gotten the habit of praying, when I can, with those who hear better than I do".[22]

These parables may seem extreme, but it happens more often than you might guess. Like many of you, I pray the Psalms. When I come to the laments, they give me better laments than my own. When I read the praise psalms, they give me doxologies strange to my tongue. I am learning to hear, though I am deaf. I am learning to sing, though I am mute. I am learning that I am fearfully and wonderfully made, though often within me a sea of accusation roars that I am not.

Today is a day of completion. A day of privileges and responsibilities accrued. Of strengths confirmed. Yet, however certain these strengths, you shall be different. By God's grace, you shall win wisdom from folly. And strength from weakness. You will see not merely with creaturely light, but with the uncreated light of God's own holy illuminations, with this light you will see. See the marks in your hands. See the wounds you carry in your heart. Hear the voice that sings our names against the crackling static of self-accusation, self-doubt, and shame: "I love you. You are mine. You shall pass through waters, through fire, through storm. But none of them will touch you. For you are mine and I have called you by name."

The One who speaks these words is the Crucified and Risen Lord. By God's grace, we will hear him.

---

22. Hoke, *Wanted*, 194.

Chapter Three

Haunted like Holy Things

"You are a church of broken glass
and hallelujahs.
You are haunted like every other
holy thing.
What tried to destroy you didn't
have the strength.
Still you stand.
Sturdy and smelling of smoke."

—Clementine von Radics

Hike through a US National Forest in late fall and mostly you won't see deer. Or if you do, you'll only see the flashing flag of the deer almost taunting you: "We saw you before you saw us!" The deer trot up along a ridge, or drop down into a ravine, disappearing into a thicket of bramble. That's it. Gone. Such a tiny glimpse of this wild thing that you scarcely grasp what these creatures are about. Don't bother trying to follow them unless you're in a National Park (and you're advised not to do that). These creatures, wild as they are, inhabit a world that is not quite the same as the world you live in, but sometimes our worlds brush against one another.

Part One: Callings

If you could find the sign of their activity when you weren't around, signs of activity when no loud humans were about, no human stink (and we do stink) to haunt a prey animal—that's interesting. Look for the scrapes. A scrape often appears in late fall, around the season that deer go into the rut, or the breeding season. Bucks will mark their territory, scraping away a thin layer of topsoil of leaves and then mark the naked soil with their own scent. You'll often see a pair of deer prints in the soft dirt, very clear as if the buck were adding its signature for good measure. Another sign of activity is to be found on a small tree, often shredded, and thrashed to pieces, where bucks have used its branches to whip and scrape the velvet from their antlers.

If you're the hunter, these signs announce that there's activity in this place. But if you're the prey . . . when we were small children, my mother took us out berry picking near the gravel pits, salmon spawning grounds, in Cordova, Alaska. She gave us our coffee cans and we had gone down a back road lined with thick blueberry bushes . . . but we didn't get very far before Mom swept all three of us up and deposited us in the cab of the truck. We were going home before we knew it. Mom told us why: she had found the bones of a freshly killed moose calf, bear prints everywhere. A grizzly was nearby.

Years ago, someone set up a camera in an eagle's nest. Everything, it was announced, had been revealed. Some indigenous people take exception to this sort of thing and maybe this is why: these animals exhibit some power of the Creator, and it is not subject to human knowing. You may know them, but only glancingly—their spirits exist to us as *blur* of eagle, but it is somehow disregarding the holy in the creature to draw too close, to become too all-knowing with something so fearfully and wonderfully made.

As in these experiences, I suspect God leaves us the sign of divine presence through verbs, verbs we often find in Scripture. There is no camera to watch God remotely, as if unobserved. But Scripture leaves us to interpret scrapes, signs of movement under cover of darkness. "Preach the verbs" is the way Anna Carter Florence put it while lecturing at the University of Dubuque Theological Seminary.

Maybe we think of the verbs as sign of God's activity. While we slept, the narrator of Genesis tells us, God created sun, moon, and stars. We do not see God so much as wake up to a world dizzy with scrapes, marks, and soil pulverized into distinctive paths of divine action. A verb feels like the spirit—or the smell, or the song in the distance, out of sight, of a great animal—as it sweeps close to you, almost by accident, and you feel not its body, but its hot breath; you hear not its words but a snuffling of Being nearby; it speaks yet without words. Everyone, including you, the Stupid Human, knows to be still, to pause, to attend to this sign of the Creator's living presence.

How might these semi-numinous experiences in creation offer a clue to the way God comes near to us as interpreters? Simone Weil describes an awe-filled withdrawal before God's living action. Preachers will sometimes depict this withdrawal using an "oblique" form of representation—it resembles the divine passive used by many of the biblical writers, obliquely signaling God's action without claiming it overtly—or the preacher's modesty in the act of interpretation.

Some forms of spirituality mistakenly exclude reading Scripture for preaching as too worldly or product oriented. Exegesis, when we see it as a regular pattern in the life with the sermon, contributes to a form of spirituality, an exegetical hunt steeped in a human experience. For the preacher, exegesis might entail technical skills but there's a feeling of communion—sometimes we feel that communion as the "distant love" of intellectual labor and at other times we feel that communion in the "heart strangely warmed." Both the "distant love" of technical and the affective dimensions of reading Scripture make for a healthy discipline of exegesis for preaching. Practically, I will share some of my experiences in the "hunt," and the "haunted," world of the preacher. How does the lens that searches for God's presence-absence draw us into the real world, the world God created for the sake of all living things? And how does that presence sometimes haunt the hunter with the holy?

Beings of Chance

In her work *Gravity and Grace*, Simone Weil writes of a landscape that exists in our human absence:

> I must withdraw so that God may make contact with the beings whom chance places in my path and whom he loves. It is tactless for me to be there. It is as though I were placed between two lovers or two friends. I am not the maiden who awaits her betrothed, but the unwelcome third who is with two betrothed lovers and ought to go away so that they can really be together. . . . May I disappear in order that those things that I see may become perfect in their beauty from the very fact that they are no longer things that

Part One: Callings

> I see.... To see a landscape as it is when I am not there.... When I am in any place, I disturb the silence of heaven and earth by my breathing and the beating of my heart.[1]

The Creator grants that Moses will only see God's backside but no more. Are the scrapes of the Creator God's way of letting us disappear in the moment of divine appearing?

Maybe we think of verbs as a form of theology *via negativa*, theology by way of the negative. A verb tells us Something passed this way once and may pass this way again. It indicates activity by way of absence. Out in the field, the hunter feels for the warmth of scat to detect proximity and time of an animal. Is the bear near or far? Is it warm? Cold? You only know the presence by way of absence and absence itself is only possible because there is presence. You may not see it, but you can, with your fingers, trace the way the bear marked out its territory. You will also be more human with the bear's absence-presence. Alert, yes, but not frozen in terror. In so doing, the verb becomes a clue about the theological direction of God, or activity, where the Spirit is going, what its purposes might be ... and how near it might be, whether it might pass this way again.

A word of caution—the God we seek does not "equal" what we expect or what we imagine. Rowan Williams, former Archbishop of Canterbury and an accomplished poet, speaks of the odd realization that "literature was actually much closer to what mattered to me about faith than what I was reading in religious studies."[2] Literature, he explains, gives us a picture of "what happens to human language in strange, borderline situations. And it does odd things. It turns on its head, does a handspring, contorts itself. It slips behind walls and puts its head over the top and waves, and sort of messes around. And I thought, that's not wholly unlike what's happening in theology."[3] In other words, theology does not begin with a narrow meaning but with an extravagant possibility, one we can only guess: "[Theological language] is not like a very dull sermon where you have to put in a few illustrations to keep people listening. Language begins with oddity and extravagance.... It makes connections far outside what you can predict."[4] So, perhaps, when we look at a story's metaphorical act of "slipping behind a wall" this points to the way language acts or behaves within the stories of Bible.

1. Weil, *Gravity and Grace*, 36–37.
2. Smith, "Obliqueness," 56.
3. Smith, "Obliqueness," 56.
4. Smith, "Obliqueness," 56.

On the other hand, I also believe the Spirit follows us. Or maybe hunts us. Those who research the behavior of bears report that they hunt the hunters, often trailing them at a distance, maybe just a few hours or a day or two separating them, apparently studying human behavior. Often the hunter doesn't even realize that it, as prey, is being stalked. Call it a "gospel of reversal" if you like. I sometimes think preachers (and congregations) are like the Stupid Hunter, ignorant prey. We imagine we are going to "find" God. But if this is a God who may be found, by the exercise of our will and faculties, what kind of God is it?

Could we liken Scripture to an ancient hunting ground, a place where generations have gone to glimpse God's work? As we read Scripture for preaching, we are, if you'll allow the expression, on a hunt, the most important hunt we can imagine, a hunt for the mystery of our existence, an indication of life's meaning, or for the assurance of our belonging. As interpreters in the Christian tradition, we trust that scriptural texts give us signs of God's presence in the world, and we also entrust ourselves to One who sought us long before we ever sought him.

More than Exegesis

"If this text were true, what kind of world would we live in?" Of the many exegetical tools one uses, this one is perhaps a must. All too often a sermon ends up being a message about how true the rotten world is and how rare the world of God is—that's too bad since it is, after all, God's world. And it gives preaching (and preachers) a bad name when we fail to convey that basic confession. It doesn't do God's reputation any good either, playing as it does into false narratives of an absentee God. The tendency to see Scripture as a blueprint for the world that does not exist makes sermons into a lot of thunder but not much lightning. Where is the living power of God in that sermon that cannot convey even a glimpse of God's living activity? Or say, "See, here, God's Spirit leads people to reconcile!"? Is the sermon to be found in the finely wrought cynicism of the one who knows better than to believe? If we aim to introduce change to the world, and most preachers do, this question asks us to awaken or exercise a sensitivity to the world as if it were alive with God's Spirit.

It also speaks to something personal. When we ask this question, we're doing more than exegesis. Or we're doing what exegesis always intended: under its guise, we conduct a short examination of our own capacity to

Part One: Callings

glimpse God's good world. Every act of healing, every narrative of peacemaking in Scripture shouts out that this is God's world. Often, in Scripture, one person stands out as needing God's healing or rescue, while others seem like bystanders. How many interpreters see themselves as whole, yet see others through the lens of disempowerment? Maybe that's me, over there, watching as if seeing, listening as if hearing ... but bereft of true sight or insight. What if the testimony of Scripture were true ... for me? What if the good news is proclaimed to those who live with despair? Or freedom came to the person in prison, really? What if it were true that the waters of adversity part and the people of God walk on dry land?

I only want you to hold out this possibility, that God's Spirit lives and acts in this world. Jesus touches the eyes of the person born blind in the Gospel of John, lathering them with spittle and mud. He tells him to go wash in the Pool of the Sent and when he returns to Jesus, he can see ... but others around him, who only moments ago saw clearly apparently cannot see: "'Is this not the man who used to sit and beg?' Some were saying, 'It is he.' Others were saying, 'No, but it is someone like him.' He kept saying, 'I am the man.' But they kept asking him, 'Then how were your eyes opened?'" (John 9:8–10). In John's telling both the person born blind and the people who "spectated" were in different degrees experiencing light. Mark's account of the person who lived with blindness feels similar. After Jesus touches his eyes, he asks, "Can you see anything?" He replies yes but maybe not quite: "I can see people, but they look like trees, walking" (Mark 8:22).

You open your eyes and what do you see? Indistinct shapes? This is often how it goes. You will want to see clearly and with continued exercise sight or insight will grow in you. But for now, if people look like trees ... isn't that one form of sight, to recognize that we haven't seen clearly and what we have seen clearly might not have been as clear as we imagined? It's been true for me. True now. The way we have viewed people in our own lives is often as fixed and static things. What if trees walked?

In John's story, the people around the man born blind saw him as fixed and static ... even though he had undergone a dramatic change, they remained the same. Or nearly. The narrator uses a sly form of irony to remind us that you can live with a visual impairment and still see, and you can see with your eyes and still be blind. John often deals in double meanings, born again/born from above being the most well-known example. Perhaps we're also to recognize that we saw this person who lived with blindness in the wooden captivity of a socially constructed diagnosis. But if the text is true, people can change; those socially constructed values can be shaken with a biblical imagination.

"Now faith is the assurance of things hoped for, the conviction of things not seen" (Heb 11:1). With these words, the preacher of Hebrews exhorts the congregation to live faith-filled lives by remembering the faith-filled actions of their ancestors. The preacher recounts generations of people who "hoped" in the reality of "things not seen"—and despite the reality that we see, still believed. Amid climate crisis, a glimpse of an ark of sustainability (11:7); Abraham, "not knowing where he was going", "set out" on a trail (11:9). The preacher's narration emphasizes, too, that sometimes the eyes of faith see beauty and dignity where others do not. This peculiar sighting gives birth to holy cunning: Moses' parents "hid" their infant "because they saw that the child was beautiful; and they were not afraid of the king's edict" (11:23); Moses chooses downward mobility over and against the contract and remunerations that Egypt promised (11:23–26). The preacher of Hebrews reconciles these two, what we can see all too clearly and what we hope for through a world governed by God's faithfulness: "By faith the people passed through the Red Sea as if it were dry land, but when the Egyptians attempted to do so they were drowned" (11:29). What if the text witnesses to the real world? Could we risk an interpretation "as if it were true" that God sustains and rescues and walks with us?

Reading the Scrapes and Signs: Examples

Scripture records that God acts in some decisive way. Look, then, for the scrapes and trails left behind by God-verbs in the scriptural tradition. Sometimes the verbs are obvious, as in Psalm 146: The Lord "made" the earth; the Lord "keeps" faith and "executes" justice; the Lord "gives food"; the Lord "liberates" and the Lord "opens"; the Lord "lifts up" and the Lord "loves"; the Lord "watches" and "upholds." The psalmist bears witness to robust actions of God on behalf of the world God so loves. Psalm 146, and the Psalms generally, do not disguise God's definitive action. Likewise, as you read Paul's letters, you hear echoes of that style of direct declaration in Jesus Christ. As Paul points to the results of justification by faith in Romans 5:5–11, we see God-agency in verbs "to pour" and "to give" (5); "to die" (6); "to prove" (8); "to save"; "to justify" (9); "to reconcile" (10); "to receive" among others. In Paul's thinking, Jesus Christ is both verb and subject, both the one who reconciles and our reconciliation (11).

Part One: Callings

Incidentally, in the interests of a more theologically grounded approach to preaching, the psalmist and epistolary writings of the New Testament offer a helpful corrective to merely "persuasive" approaches to preaching that speak to our human experience. Probably dating to the "narrative turn" in theology, Pauline texts were set to one side as too "abstract" or doctrinal for contemporary ways of thinking. That's a loss. Paul isn't abstract. Paul shares a kindred spirit with the psalmist as well as to the prophets, especially as they speak directly to or lay claim on God's saving actions, and in Paul's case Jesus' saving significance. What's the value of leaving that language behind? The Gospel writers depended on the psalmist and Paul as significant backdrops for how they came to interpret the saving significance of Jesus' life—does that not also inform us as well?

But this is also true: it is easier to preach from a narrative than it is to preach from a psalm or an ancient Pauline argument. Why? Are they too direct? Is it because the God-verbs, as I call them, blaze across the page? Maybe. I hope from time to time you will practice your skills as an interpreter by preaching from a psalm (or a writing from Paul) as your primary text. However, the norm for preaching is probably a story; indeed, even when preaching from a psalm, the psalmist's song evokes a story which is purposely ambiguous in the text itself, thus inviting us to tell our story. Intentional ambiguity on the part of the psalmist acts as a tender invitation to the reading community to tell its story or to let the psalm tell the story of the Other in our midst. Maybe that's for another book.

When you have a story that makes no pretense except to be a story, you will study the verbs as they appear relative to other agents in the text, protagonists, antagonists, and so on. However, the primary protagonist in Scripture is God alone, and almost always the text bears witness to God's agency, even when it doesn't appear that God is doing anything at all. You "discover" God's agency as protagonist (and perhaps as antagonist!) in the verbs of the text, but you need to look at the text with a theological lens.

In the worldview of Scripture, all verbs belong to God. Daniel's account of the fall of Judah to King Nebuchadnezzar underlines this God-anchored worldview, even when it seems to go against God: "The Lord let King Jehoiakim of Judah fall into [King Nebuchadnezzar's] power" (Dan 1:2). This is an example of the divine passive. Without saying so outright, the writer tells us that despite all evidence to the contrary, God is the agent at work in the text. This is especially true in the narrative genre. God "lets" agents that are ostensibly opposed to God become unwitting agents of

Haunted like Holy Things

God's historical purpose. That purpose includes not only granting success but also verbs conferring defeat. This may seem difficult to reconcile with God's enemies being, well, God's enemies. But in the economy of salvation, God triumphs over every enemy, so that even God's enemies who work to undermine God's purposes are, indeed, already instruments of God's salvific purpose. It is this logic that allows Bonhoeffer to conclude that Judas Iscariot did more to advance Jesus' cause than all the actions of the faithful put together.

As you look at the verbs in a pericope, experiment with how they evoke not only the agents directly at work in each text but how they depict God as the radical protagonist. Mark's story of the friends who carry the paralytic to the house where Jesus is teaching provides a demonstration of the "indirect" depictions of God's saving activity through Jesus of Nazareth. On the surface of Mark 2:1–12, Jesus does very little. Mark says that Jesus "was at home" and he was "speaking the word" to the people. Mark gives two verses to Jesus' activity, which is homebound and teacherly. The writer hints at something afoot in saying that Jesus "speaks the word" but where, in the narrative, do we hear the energy of this text? Not in an amazing sermon but in the disruptive grunt-work of the four people who carry their paralyzed friend to Jesus. We detect it as well perhaps in concrete challenge posed by paralysis: the wall of a crowd separating the sick one from Jesus may seem like the least of their problems.

Curiously, Mark allows us to forget stubborn paralysis, at least for a moment. Maybe it's the way the Markan narrator deploys verbs. When the four people carrying their friend try to gain entrance through the front of the house, they can't get in. They scratch their heads, "What to do?" "I know," says one. "Let's get him up on the roof and see if we can't find a soft spot in it. We'll dig a hole and lower him down so the healer can't help but see him." More grunting. Yelling. Heaving. Now they start clawing through the roof, bits of dried clay falling onto the heads of people below. You get the idea. The verbs tell the story: to carry, to remove, to dig, to let down.

A nontheological reading of this text will underscore presenting themes like human teamwork, determination, overcoming the odds, improvisation, etc. But a theological reading might point to Jesus who, strangely enough, is in the room or at home in the world. How did he get there? Think back to Mark's introduction of Jesus in 1:9–13. The Spirit's grand entrance during Jesus' baptism includes these verbs: to tear apart; to descend, to drive. Jesus is acted on, but he is not, at present, the actor.

Part One: Callings

The heavens were torn apart, and heaven fell like a dove onto the heads of humankind. What does it take to tear through a thick roof in an ancient house? Quite a lot, to be sure. What does it take for God to become human, full of grace and truth, to tear through the barrier separating sinners from the announcement of God's good news? Could the dust of heavenly unrest and determination be the startling way the Spirit activates Jesus as preacher and savior? Could this be a clue to one of the major theological claims within this text, albeit in the indirect witness of the four people who carry their paralyzed friend to Jesus?

Another interesting possibility might exist in the idea that Jesus enters our "world" the way this person with paralysis enters—he enters with power revealed through perfect weakness. Race forward sixteen chapters, and perhaps we see that this text foreshadows the narrative of resurrection: "But [the angelic figure] said to them, 'Do not be alarmed; you are looking for Jesus of Nazareth, who was crucified. He has been raised; he is not here. Look, there is the place they laid him. But go, tell his disciples and Peter that he is going ahead of you to Galilee; there you will see him, just as he told you'" (Mark 16:6–7).

In the following example, my assignment was to preach from the passage in Luke where Mary goes to see Elizabeth, the fourth text assigned in Advent (Year C). That this is an Advent season text is really a note for you, as pastoral theologian who cares about the seasons, rather than the beginning of your sermon. Our assignment is not Advent, but biblical interpretation for preaching. Dive into the text.

So, that's what I did. What did I find? I found four verbs: got up, went, entered, and called out.

Luke loves this sort of thing, insinuating the story of salvation into vanishingly insignificant acts. The writer does it with the story of the good Samaritan, using verbs freighted with Christ's saving significance: "But a Samaritan, while traveling came near him . . ." (Luke 10:33). This Samaritan is not a subject so much as a series of movements in the economy of God's saving love. The Samaritan sees, moves, goes, bandages, pours, puts, brings, cares, takes, gives, promises.

Compare those verbs to the priest and Levite. The priest goes, sees, and passes. The Levite goes, sees, and passes. Blink and you'd miss them entirely. Why is that style of storytelling important? Luke tells us a story and, importantly, teaches us *how* to tell the story of good news. Take your time, the Lukan writer seems to say, linger over the action, its peculiarities. The writer of Luke slows to a crawl whenever depicting the gospel as action—why should we rush the gospel? And, perhaps important for preachers, why would we linger overlong on the stupidity of our society? Our society is no less hypocritical than Luke's but in Luke's story, hypocrisy is only a bit of stage prop, not the central thing.

Note to self: for the next sermon, see the good and linger with it.

Back to Elizabeth and Mary. We almost always find ourselves in Mary's Magnificat, with big, rambling actions of a God who sweeps up the wicked, feeds the poor good things, and sends the rich home empty. Great song. Mary's song (or possibly Elizabeth's—you could make a case that the tradition is wrong on this one) is a beautiful climax in which Luke brings together these two women and their parallel pregnancies.

If this were a musical score, maybe we would hear a barely detectable sound, a single key, Mary gets up, then another, goes, slowly rising to a sprinkle of sound accumulating (the greetings) eventually into the climax of 47–55 and then returning to the almost quiet place in 56: "And Mary remained with her about three months and then returned to her home."

That preamble seemed important to me. In two short verses, Mary gets up (or rose up), goes, enters, and cries out to Elizabeth.

Maybe it struck me as important because of what a woman said in a support group that I belong to. This didn't make it into the sermon, but it was one of those irritants that made me think about the courage in this simple act, getting up. The interpretive irritant in my support group wasn't a young woman who figuratively "got up" but an elderly woman who suffered from chronic pain making it almost impossible for her to sit down. I knew her from previous meetings, and she was a regular but not lately. It's the pain, she told us, it made it excruciating for her to sit down for any length of time. But she said that being with us meant more to her than the discomfort, that was why she was there that night. She might not be with us the next, but this night, she was there. Her testimony helped me see in these seemingly insignificant acts verbs as clues to a quality of spirit valued by Luke.

I also began to see the twin pregnancies of Luke as "high-risk" pregnancies. This insight was brought home for me by the work of a midwife activist, Ruth Weston. Her fight to put women at the center of the birthing experience, rather than institutions and medical professionals, came to mind:

> Do not assume that we birthed our brains with our baby, and that because we have lost our economic status our knowledge and opinion have likewise lost their value. I did not ditch my academic brain

when I became a mother, nor my scientific training nor my speaking skills. My brain may leak out of my boobs sometimes but there is plenty left and I am the subject not the object of your care.[5]

Again, this sharp-witted insight did not make it into the sermon (but now that I'm reading it, maybe it should have!), but this fellow pilgrim seems to get these two women and their "high-risk" pregnancies in a way that was more existential and human than if I had only consulted my experience (limited to be sure), a commentary, or only read them as "biblical" women.

Luke privileges their voices and their actions, much like a liberationist midwife might praise and hold up the courage, tenacity, and audacity of women who insist on care that recognizes women's experience and intelligence in the story of childbirth. Weston's context is the institutionalization of childbirth. Luke's context might be different, but the impulse of courageous unrest is something that they share.

I was also struck that the birth story as we have it really begins not with the birth of John the Baptist or even Jesus (you may not want to push that one too far—or too little), but the birth of Elizabeth as a prophet. Important. Jesus' presence in utero already signals the beginning of the new age, the prophecy of Joel outdone: Your old *women* shall prophesy! Luke reports that Elizabeth "heard" Mary's greeting—and what she heard! She heard the mother of her Lord, the child leaped in her womb (that's the testimony of a third person confirming that this is in fact a divine word rather than something else), and she was filled with the Holy Spirit. Luke reports in this compact scene on the birth of a prophet in Elizabeth, an elderly woman, an elderly *pregnant* woman, in a patriarchal society that has pushed her and her high-risk pregnancy to the margins.

Now about Mary. She got up. I found myself trying to connect Mary's song to Mary's pedestrian actions in v. 39, "she got up". It's hard to do. Maybe it's impossible. Maybe my own predilection is to say that Mary knew all along, because, after all, she is a *biblical* woman. No. She is a human being and Luke doesn't tell us that she got up ready to sing the Magnificat. She got up to go see Elizabeth. Purpose. That's it. Or is it? Imagine, if we can, the difficulty of this simple movement—she heaved herself up.

Message in and through the verbs: God takes such efforts, however small in scale, and multiplies the action into something like an alternative world, an altered imagination of who we are because of whose we are.

---

5. Ruth Weston, unpublished manuscript.

The riff that I came up with suited the purpose that was developing for the message, and it went something like this: "When Mary got up, do you imagine she was thinking that, Today, justice will flow like a mighty stream? Or that today, the poor will be fed good things and the rich will go away empty? Or that today, every tear would be wiped away and there would be no more suffering? Or that today, nations would learn war no more and a little child would lead them? We don't know. We do know that Mary's purpose that day had a name, and her name was Elizabeth."

Keeping It Real

Mining a text for its indirect or direct suggestion of God's agency as protagonist in the salvation story will be crucial to any sermon you subsequently develop. Equally important, you will want to consider how people of faith might respond to that theological claim. What does it mean that God enters the world in a manner that would seem to have more in common with a person who lives with seemingly devastating disability or through the experience of women in high-risk pregnancies? How might attending to these human conditions or our views of people who live with at risk of their gender change our experience of Jesus who "succumbs" to the radical disability of the cross, death, and tomb?

One rule of interpreting Scripture is that often when we "see" the sick, we are only seeing the most visibly sick. And in some ways, to the extent that the sick know their sickness, e.g., the woman with the twelve-year hemorrhage, she is healthier than those who imagine that they are doing just fine. She knows she needs healing and trusts that Jesus holds the power of her healing. And she acts on that knowledge, and even Jesus is surprised. The point is that we all have need of God's healing and part of our task as interpreters is to see how the Scripture diagnoses our sickness with God's healing.

We're talking about the formation of human identity in "conformity" with Christ. Practically, this points to what counts as a "faithful response" to a given theological claim. In terms of homiletical craft, this human response goes under different names. Tom Long describes it as the "claim of the text" and how that claim affects or changes the intended audience. Put another way, the theological content of the text places a lien on our worldview. Paul Scott Wilson dubs it the "human need" relative to the theme and doctrine suggested by the text. James Harris, a student of Samuel Proctor, might say that the "relevant question" raised by the theological claim of the text is addressed to the world as it is, so that it may be conformed to God's peaceable rule rather than the rule of the violent. Eugene Lowry usually identifies the human response in stages of discovery, beginning with an itch. For Lowry, the need is never simply psychological but always a narratively shaped, gospel-driven itch that leads to a celebration. Others, perhaps influenced by a pastoral approach to preaching, might say that the need is the human thirst suggested by the text: what human hurt, ache, dysfunction does this God seem to address? And how?

As we think about the formation of human community in the *imago dei*, especially with ideas of Jesus' incarnation as inhabiting the human body, subject as it always is to limits (some more obvious than others) we want to exercise care that we name a theology of giftedness. In this, we think of disability—and by implication, incarnation—as not exceptional but the truest thing about us. We are human. God became as we are and, in the incarnation, exceptionally visible as limited rather than unlimited.

Charles Campbell calls this exercise "dislocated exegesis" because we go outside the physical church to read—I call it missiological exegesis, doing our reading where God "sends" the Word, because that's where God forms the church. As the "dislocated" it is radically located. Interpreters who undertake a christological pilgrimage become, in the world's view, undocumented, almost naked. That is, if you go to a grocery store, your "documents" might be the car you drove in, the way you dress, your personal wealth, and your ethnicity. But what if your only document was something that had no value in that place? Or the way you are "marked" prevented your free movement in that place? What if you were to read texts about hunger in aisles lined with food?

When I first gave my students this assignment, missiological exegesis, i.e., asking them to step outside their comfort zone and do their exegesis in a non-church environment, a few of them went to Starbucks. Some of them also imagined I was asking them to read these texts out to people in these settings as an evangelical exercise, seeking converts. Not quite. What I was hoping to spark was a contextual discovery, that Scripture read in a context can be disclosive, even apocalyptic, as reading a text in a "hot space" uncovers realities that we take as given, exposing us to difference, perhaps opening us to the experience of others because in that moment we share physical space.

Haunted like Holy Things

So, I became more specific with "acceptable" locations for exegetical pilgrimages: a city dump; an emergency room at the hospital; a funeral home; a nursing home; a shelter for survivors of domestic violence; outside a CEO's office (see how long it takes for security to escort you off the property); find and use a pair of crutches and read the text with the experience of limited mobility; visit a methadone clinic; or join an AA group and admit your own brokenness and desire to be healed.

Other contexts deaden us, and they are everywhere. Walmart. McDonald's. Amazon Fulfillment Centers. The waiting area in an international airport at 2:17 AM. The nonstop drone of CNN or Fox News in the hotel lobby. What, in the latter location, might it be like to read the Beatitudes of Matthew 5:1–16?

Bonhoeffer speaks approvingly of Friedrich Nietzsche's idea that we ought to love the farthest. Loving our neighbor, he says, has led people in the church to imagine God only in the protected space of proximity. Missiological exegesis lets us follow the verbs in places where we might feel as if God's Word were excluded or, by cultural structures, rendered meaningless or invisible.

A group of Catholic Workers make an annual pilgrimage to a bank in downtown Chicago. Outside they set up tables where they hand out sweet rolls and coffee, free of charge, as a witness to the God who came as bread for the hungry, without cost and without money. In so doing, they move from "reading" to "performing" Christ in a place where it seems God's promises stop.

None of this will necessarily give you the sermon—but these kinds of activities, from considering the verbs, to thinking about the images of God conveyed in the verbs and the corresponding images of human community, to missiological exegesis of the text (and maybe occasionally its performance) will help as you formulate a controlling idea for the sermon.

It is neither the sermon nor is it not the sermon. It is the ground you're standing on . . . and it might be holy.

Part One: Callings

Signposts for the Footpath

On July 5, 2018, a young girl, Taylor Hayes, was shot in Baltimore. The bullet wasn't intended for her. Shootings are too common in Baltimore but when children are the victims, it strikes a nerve. We had been active as a church in the movement to reduce gun violence, working with grassroots organizations in the inner city to address the systemic racism that contributed to this as well as to empower communities to speak their truths to people in power for better policing and community care.

Even with that, I felt that my routine places (home or church study) were too far removed from Taylor's world, who at that moment was hooked up to life-support in the ICU of the Baltimore Trauma Center. The Trauma Center was about two miles walk from the church. I took my notebook, my Bible, and went.

Finally at the hospital, I was physically closer to Taylor, a few floors away, but curiously I felt the distance, almost more than I did "at home" in my routine spaces. She was the human equivalent of a crime scene and being in the hospital only accentuated that reality. I sat at an open table in the hospital cafeteria. I opened my Bible to the text I would be preaching on that Sunday, Luke's account of Jesus' crucifixion. Luke's account interrogated me in a way that I had not anticipated: "But all of Jesus' acquaintances, including the women who had followed him from Galilee, stood at a distance, watching these things" (23:49).

Reading that text, without a context to frame it, it had felt as if the narrator was judging Jesus' acquaintances, and the women too. But with Taylor nearby and yet distant, I found something different: maybe the women and those who follow Jesus watched, helpless and yet with tenderness. Luke's narrator presents women in a tender light, perhaps even here in the hour of Jesus' death. I did not want to be helpless—that, in truth, was one part of my motive for coming. But Luke asks me to consciously join those who watch these things, to be helpless, and in a manner to draw near to the helpless in our shared humanity.

Taylor Hayes died on July 19, 2018. She was seven years old.

PART TWO

Tinkering

Chapter Four

Creature Comforts

"When you come, bring the cloak that I left with Carpus at Troas, also the books, and above all the parchments."

—2 Timothy 4:13

When we moved to the United Kingdom in late 2020, we chose to liquidate everything we owned rather than box our possessions up for a journey across the Atlantic. Most things can be replaced. Except for what we could fit into six large suitcases and the small carry-ons we were allowed, we either sold, donated, or gave away virtually everything we had acquired over the course of our days here on earth. It was a little like dying. Especially difficult for me were the books. Some of the books felt like life-marks: I was in this place when I read this book. Other collections represented different stages of my intellectual life. I still think about that as a massive loss. But when it came to a ten-volume set of biblical commentaries (plus some others that I had collected over the years), I packed these into two of our six large suitcases. While I did not know what the future held, if it included preaching (and it has), I felt the strong need for these books. They're not books that I exactly enjoy reading or that fill me with sentiment, like my old copy of John Steinbeck's *East of Eden*. Instead, they form the basis of a large part of my intellectual life, as a preacher—and I felt that I could not be without them, whatever the future might have entailed.

Those books, and a sermon I heard years ago riffing on 2 Timothy 4:13, "only remember the parchments"—they resonated: the preacher called us to the centrality of wisdom and teaching in the preaching moment. Our context was a group of professors, teachers of preachers. And it was a winning theme, then as it is now. But the preacher did not spend as much time on the "cloak"—or what I would call the creature comforts of the preacher. The "my cloak, also the books, and especially the parchments" pattern shows up in Dietrich Bonhoeffer's letters from prison. Lines like this are typical: "In my own reading I now live entirely in the nineteenth century. During these past months I have read Gotthelf, Stifter, Immermann, Fontaine, and Keller with renewed admiration."[1] Readers glimpse in these fragments an inspiring theologian, capable of carrying on with many, many books, not least his daily Bible reading. Bonhoeffer speaks of books as friends for whose welfare he is concerned, almost as if they were living companions, as we hear him speaking to his parents: "From my books I would like to have Vilmar, Schlatter, Calvin stored someplace safe, perhaps also the old pictures in my room, but please do not take too much trouble with this. Books can always be acquired again later."[2] Bonhoeffer links his books to more ordinary comforts: "When it's convenient, I would like to get Hoskyn's *Riddle of the New Testament* (stands on the shelf above my bed), also some cotton wool since it is sometimes noisy at night."[3] While on the one hand, he says the "physical needs are completely secondary and unimportant"—probably said more to assure his parents than as a true statement of his conditions in prison—on the other hand, his letters often end with postscripts like this one: "At some point, could you please drop off the following items for me here: slippers, shoelaces (long, black), shoe polish, stationary and envelopes, ink, tobacco ration card, shaving soap, as well as sewing kit and another suit to change into?"[4] Elsewhere, Bonhoeffer ponders on what a prisoner has written on the wall, "A hundred years from now, none of this will matter"—another stark reminder of his radical displacement from anything home and, equally, the way the familiar becomes unfamiliar in a new context.

1. Bonhoeffer, *Letters and Papers*, 120.
2. Bonhoeffer, *Letters and Papers*, 131.
3. Bonhoeffer, *Letters and Papers*, 99.
4. Bonhoeffer, *Letters and Papers*, 57.

Creature Comforts

Books exist as companions to the preaching life. But alongside these books are what I call the "creature comforts" or the way in which the root narratives of the biblical world find new life not by being original but by being recast in new mediums, new modes perhaps even in prison. All this is to say that I'm not interested in dropping the book pack in an indifferent way, as if everything we learned in seminary was a mistake or somehow interferes with the disclosure of our true self in preaching, whatever that is. Instead, this chapter recasts the role of parchment and cloak from the point of view of the footpath, how its different settings can reconceive these resources for the vocation. While not disavowing the profound complexity of the preaching life, or the preacher's indebtedness to the theological disciplines, I do make a case for reshaping the burden of the preacher so that it is fitting to their life rather than the other way around. Specifically, I think in these terms: the place of bricolage, books, and what I call the "creature comforts" of the preacher's life.

The Bricoleur

Preaching feels different as an intellectual exercise—it feels different because it is different. While our sermons benefit from rigorously applied methodologies of theological and biblical scholarship, the preacher's life finds itself most at home in the slightly chaotic art of bricolage, the practice of bringing seemingly unrelated, ephemeral, and miscellaneous phenomena into a coherent interpretation of the human experience. Bricolage comes from the French verb *bricoler* ("to tinker"). Intuitive associations, metaphor, drawing connections that might be surprising or unexpected, randomly salvaged, kept or discarded, picked up again, turned upside down and inside out until it sparks something . . . or, if it doesn't, set aside for another day when it does. Preachers are endlessly attracted to seemingly insignificant events or experiences that, oddly but memorably, help us to see Jesus. This singular preoccupation is what distinguishes a preacher from other artists or perhaps it is our singular focus, our life-theme.

The preacher may have a library and that is good, but the lively sermon draws on seeming miscellany, ephemera that seem perfectly at home not only in the artist's studio but in congregational preaching—the art of bricolage comes from a habitus of listening for the "still small voice" as we cultivate a sensitivity to the holy in ordinary life. Bricolage testifies to the unmethodological spirit of the poet who, seeing the black shadow of flight in a different direction, turns to see where it leads, where our future is not known but entrusted to the Spirit who beckons us to continue, perhaps in another direction. Maybe this is what it means for me, like that bird. Why is it going in a different direction? Is it leading me or signing me to an alternative path?

A piece or a story does not always come fully formed or clear cut for the preacher. Often, it sits there, complicated and interesting, like the piece of plastic that you find in your desk, and it seems important, designed with gaps and insets, but you have no idea what for—a story may be like that, its attachments or associations vague. A better analogy would be a piece of driftwood: you get the feeling of something familiar or strange in familiarity, or just a slight curiosity but not a clear connection. You carry it with you, absentmindedly. It is not so much possession as freeloader, keeping you as its own, a drifter with no place to go or no place to call home.

Why is naming the art of bricolage important? Seeing Jesus may be our peculiar art—our studio floor littered, and its walls festooned with odd bits and bobs—but sometimes our exegetical plans seem to ignore this basic aspect of preaching. Exegetical plans and homiletical maps offer a conceptually neat way of thinking about preaching. Gardner C. Taylor once said that we should begin with something familiar to us. Would he also recognize the "familiar" as the ordinary? The exegetical plan that I used for my students was *not* the one I had learned to use as a preacher. In my practice, I began with something intuitional and sometimes it grew right and sometimes it just grew wild. A formal exegetical plan asks us to identify the text, say what it means (in a few sentences), and then asks the interpreter to exegete the text through the biblical, theological, and contextual lenses and finally apply a claim of the text, focus and function. Very academic, orderly, and mostly good. But I never felt honest about the art of the preacher, which isn't nearly as neat as most exegetical plans imply. On the other hand, using a formal exegetical plan has probably saved me a lot of time (and my congregations some puzzlement) in the text to sermon journey.

However, I'll keep the zigzag, hints and guesses, hunches, and stalls of the bricoleur—if we by faith seek understanding, everything is potentially aflame with holy fire. We only need to turn to see it. Bricolage appears to surface in the oddest sorts of things:

- a baby blackbird that I rescued when it fell out of its nest and raised for a while, until, after we released it—it then began dive bombing the bald men in our hamlet;

- using the manuscript of last week's sermon to build a fire;
- when my daughter nearly ran me over as she sprinted through the living room, and I said, "no running in the house" to which she replied, "I'm not running—I'm *jogging*!"
- that night we were looking for the Boggle Hole Youth Hostel and we passed (but did not see) the sign that said, "No Cars Beyond this Point" and nearly drove into the North Sea at high tide.

They seem random and nonsensical. But each of them unlocked something for the interpretive moment. Potentially, ordinary things or experiences "do" the revealing at a slant, whereas if we tried to do it directly, it would be dull.

Sermons often become homes to things that seem purely ephemeral—a person who preaches regularly can almost see their sermons as a personal journal. But if that's the case, why not keep a journal to record these everyday events? Good idea. Mostly what you write doesn't rise to the level of the sermon. As a practice, however, a journal nudges you to recall the day's little surprises, the simplicity of its wisdom. If we don't pay attention to the little signs of grace, blindness, or tragedy, we will not be able to convey the greater tragedies or the greater grace of the Spirit as it sanctifies our world.

The following was preached the Sunday after the AME Church shooting in Charleston, South Carolina on June 17, 2015. It contains bricolage of tragedy by means of which the sermon invited the congregation to think about the more difficult problem of White denial:

> Yesterday afternoon, I was left alone with our two-year-old and so, because there was a break in the weather and the house was feeling cramped, I took her on a walk to a park not far from our house. On the way over, I looked ahead of us to see a baby bird, an apparently dead chick on the sidewalk, probably blown out of its nest in the weather that was passing through. This is always a sad sight, something I was glad that our two-year-old did not see. But there was something different and it took me a moment to see what I was seeing, something right and wrong at the same time: the mother of the bird was atop its chick, as if its baby were still in her nest, trying to keep it warm, even though it had obviously died. As I approached, it crouched, watching me, and finally succumbing to nature and instinct, flew away. When I came back, twenty minutes later, the mother robin had not returned.
>
> I share this image with you because it strikes me that the nine who were killed in the Charleston AME Church are the church's daughters and sons, our own kin. Stricken by racism, shattered

by gun shots, tossed to the ground, bodies deformed by savagery inspired by stupidity and ignorance—they may seem far from us, but in fact, we are kin to them and they to us through baptism. In a sense, this church, your congregation, is just one part of a much larger movement, a movement that gathered them as it has gathered us. But I am afraid that sometimes an ordinary robin has more motherly instinct than we do. It would be too easy to abandon the dead, to forget them, or to imagine that this is somehow so far removed from our lives as people of the church, that it does not impinge on us, not on us personally, or to let this news run its natural and inevitable course, finally exhausting itself in meaninglessness.[5]

Bricolage does not simply say, "This is what it means." Nor does it rise very high in its value to the world except perhaps for you—in it you glimpsed the world or God or both. It feels small, something easily forgotten. And yet it is these sorts of ephemera that probe the intensely complex feelings we have about life and death, our relationships to those we love, and those we treat as strangers because they are different in complexion or land.

It may not be that bricolage comes to you as an "on-time delivery"—keeping a personal journal, with just a note or two about something that happened that day, something that made you know that you're alive—these forms of bricolage give the basis for a thanksgiving that we recognize. "Room 320," a poem by John-Paul Flintoff, teaches us how we experience love in ordinary paths:

> If you get the bus towards
>   Maryleborne Station, it's just a short
>   walk
>   to the psychiatric hospital.
> If you ring the bell,
> and they let you in, say you've come
>   to see the man in Room 320
> If you go up to the third floor
>   you'll probably find
>   his door is open. They're keeping
>   watch.
> If he looks (as he will)
>   depressed and anxious
>   tell him this before you leave:
> You are loved.[6]

---

5. See full text by Robert Hoch, "Peculiar Instinct," 98–106.
6. Flintoff, *Psalms for the City*, Kindle ed. loc. 161.

The poet takes us along pathways that seem insignificant and yet, with each set of directions, the weight of longing grows—without the ephemera that litters the sidewalk nothing like the ache for belonging could ever be known. Or it feels like just another day, another meaningless journey . . .

The Books

The dean of St. Mary's Ecumenical Institute, a nearby seminary, extended a special invitation to Baltimore preachers for a "private audience" with a noted biblical scholar who was in town for a lecture. We arrived at the appointed time. We made a quick stop at the table set with pastries, bagels, fruit, and coffee. Plates held delicately in our laps, we introduced ourselves. The scholar opened the discussion by asking a question: "So how do you use commentaries in your work as preachers? Do you find them helpful?"

We mostly gave the kinds of answers you might expect while in the company of a respected biblical scholar, e.g., how we use the commentaries, when, perhaps the types of commentary we prefer, and maybe the books of the Bible we've been preaching from or whether we were using the lectionary. So on and so forth. Then one of us blurted it out: "When I'm reading the commentaries, I feel like I'm in a desert." Our circle went very quiet. He sounded genuinely heartbroken. The biblical scholar stammered, feeling torn perhaps between a pastoral instinct and maybe a little defensive, too. The scholar insisted that the guild had tried to be more accessible to preachers, that there had been improvements, before adding that there wasn't much more that biblical scholars could do. And then we went on to other topics—not because the pastor's concern was lacking in importance or because it was only true for one pastor, but maybe because neither scholar nor practitioner knew quite how to name the problem that confronted us: a commentary doesn't feel like anything likely to "feed" us. And yet, we don't feel right about preaching without the company of biblical scholars.

Someone might say that scholars don't write commentaries to supply a preacher with sermons. Of course, we all knew that. I'm putting it baldly, but it begs the question: What kind of book is the commentary? Do the biblical scholars serve as the adjudicators of meaning? Or can they serve as a friendly irritant or provide the service of clarification? Do those who live with the sermon read a commentary the way they might read a book, from beginning to end? Or is it primarily a tool which helps the reader "solve problems" related to the text?

Part Two: Tinkering

Commentaries and sermons feel like they come from different planets. During my doctoral studies, I witnessed this gulf firsthand, as a noted scholar in biblical studies sent an unsolicited exegetical guide for preaching (twenty-five pages long) to another senior member of the Practical Theology Department—it never saw the light of day. At the seminary where I eventually taught homiletics, I proposed an interdisciplinary approach to preaching, drawing on the scholarship and teaching approaches represented by two fields of theological enquiry, homiletics and biblical studies. It was killed in committee by a senior member of the Bible faculty. Even though preachers are the single largest user of commentaries and biblical scholars are the single largest producers of commentaries, these two seem to be very distinct from one another and, in some cases, adversarial.

Many preachers struggle with the commentary and its role in preaching. The "desert" experience shared above is one many would recognize. Others feel their own interpretations are flimsy compared to the dense readings of a scholar, a lifetime's worth of immersion into the study of probably that one book. Still others may not quite know how to use a commentary whether as a tool to solve a technical problem or something bigger. A few preachers worship at the feet of the biblical scholar, citing their arguments as if they were consulting divine beings. As one who values these sorts of resources, I wanted to think about why and how and for whom I use these resources. What follows are some thoughts about "how to read" commentaries as one who lives with the congregational sermon.

For those of us who preach, opening a commentary is almost like Thomas, who says, "Let us also go, that we may die with him"—that is, if we open a biblical commentary, you may well be risking your sermonic life. You will have similar experiences. I won't say that every time I open a commentary my initial ideas (my sermonic darlings) are terminated by biblical scholars. But it happens enough that it strikes me as interesting. Something dies in every journey from text to sermon; and maybe something dies before something else (and something better) can come to fruition.

In truth, what happens more often than the "termination of my darlings" is a nuancing of my adolescent enthusiasms, and by that, I mean I begin to see the latent, sometimes sparkling intelligence of the Spirit lurking just beneath the surface of my murky hunches. There lies the importance of the commentary for the preacher. It is not the Almighty Preacher Corrector (or Sermon Killer) but a conversation that you eavesdrop on—if you've used your native intelligence, living in and with the text, you're already engaged but maybe not quite a member of the invited group presupposed by a biblical scholar. Think of the commentary as a massive data leak that very few people can wade through. As you track down your story, you look for the footprints and fingerprints of your sermonic hunch. You wade into this information dump—like a scavenger, a scrap-seeker.

Use biblical commentaries like the birds that go through the seed I leave in their feeder: they flick away what seems from my point of view to be tons of valuable stuff, but they don't want it. To get quickly and efficiently at what they do want, they fling seeds into the wind with abandon. They show little or no concern for my effort in putting stuff out for their benefit. They know what they want, and they go for it. Yet, something happens between the "seed dump" and later in the day: I see these same birds picking through the remains, things that escaped their interest but now, in a different hour, feel promising.

I cannot tell you how many times I have taken exhaustive notes and, later, remembered a phrase or an insight that I had merely passed over in the first reading and later hungered for as the key concept—and like one of our birds late in the day, you'd see me hopping from page to page, or picking through the tangled scrawl of my notes, looking for that line, that turn of phrase, knowing that it was thrown away in my initial feasting. Changing metaphors, biblical commentary often contains a memorable turn of phrase that lodges itself in the interpreter's thinking. It sits there like a friendly irritant, to chew on, or brood with. Only this week, a commentary remarked that the Spirit's arrival in Acts 2 was "a noisy affair"—did I note it first thing? No, it was late in the day, and I returned looking for remnants.

Use commentaries for information in the short term and formation in the long term. Formational approaches to the commentary represent a commitment to learning the biblical world of a book as opposed to preaching episodically on a pericope that happens to grab your attention. When I'm using a commentary in the formational mode, I deliberately keep the sermonic idea at a distance. I learn Luke or John or the narrative cycles of Abraham and Sarah. In formation mode, I feel as if I'm "learning other languages" for God by immersion into the biblical world of say, Proverbs, or one of the laments. Live for a few minutes a day with a scholar who studies Psalms.

If I were to try to replicate each week the reading of the text that a scholar gives, I would give maybe one sermon a month. A sturdy volume by a thoughtful reader of the texts supports a healthy diet of preaching and it doesn't cheat me (or the congregation) out of meaningful pastoral care and congregational life.

Speaking about commentary writing, one biblical scholar said that her work on John felt like an "information dump—you start at 1.1 and you're done at 21:25." Regardless of how lacking in complexion are such texts, we need to keep in mind the communities kept by the biblical scholar. They may not be shouted out loud, but they inform the commentator's thinking. These communities include classroom, guild, church, as well as interpretive locations, for example feminist scholars or scholars who live with disabilities.

Generally, commentaries are not "thesis-driven," as in to argue a feminist interpretation or a theory of disability. However, the sympathies of biblical scholars, and the communities they keep, surface in their work even in a series like the Anchor Bible, famous for hewing closely to the text, or avoiding "thesis-driven" commentary.[7] Compare, for instance, how Jeremy Schipper, whose interests include disability theology, views the role of chance in Ruth versus the traditional view of the invisible guiding hand of God which is assumed by Edward F. Campbell Jr. Both write their commentary on Ruth for the Anchor Bible, making it an interesting case study.

According to Campbell, Ruth 2:3 creates a particular problem, which he captures in his translation of the text: "So [Ruth] set out and came and gleaned in the field after the harvesters. Now her *luck* brought her to the plot of the field belonging to Boaz."[8] Schipper's translation is similar: "When she went and gleaned in the field behind the harvesters, she *chanced* upon the portion of the field held by Boaz."[9] Campbell's commentary asserts that "God is the only person present in all of the scenes, but always in the shadows." He points to this text as an example, claiming that this is not about "luck" but in fact about God's divine hand moving in the background: "the audience knows it is hardly chance that Ruth came to Boaz' field."[10]

In Schipper, by contrast, we see a scholar thinking about the randomness of things and coming to conclude that the writer may not intend a God-in-the-shadows but something else: "By chance, Ruth gleans in Boaz's field. Although generally all events were thought to be controlled by divine forces in the ancient Near East, the text does not provide evidence that this

---

7. Schipper, *Ruth*, 28.
8. Campbell Jr., *Ruth*, 85.
9. Schipper, *Ruth*, 116.
10. Campbell Jr., *Ruth*, 112.

chance event indicates specifically YHWH's providence."[11] In his introduction, he sets out his case against the traditional "theological reading of Ruth" particularly as put forward by Ronald M. Hals, whose work has influenced many scholars, including Campbell. This idea insisted on a divine hand guiding each particular event in Ruth. Schipper says that to some extent the presence of God's hand in the story is in the eye of the beholder since God only appears to be active in terms of fertility of field and womb. He adds: "It is not that the narrator hides God behind human activities or that Ruth's pregnancy is the culmination of a chain of events guided by divine providence, but that the narrator does not credit God with activities that humans can control on their own."[12] For Schipper, looking for an "invisible hand" or a God-in-the-Shadows inflates God's actions even as we miss the quality of the divine *in* human actions: "Just because a relatively short book does not attribute many actions to God does not mean that those actions are hidden. The portrayal of divine activity in Ruth comes through in the quality of divine actions, not the quantity."[13]

Closer to our sermonic desk is *Interpretation*, a series written with the preacher's work in view. Katharine Doob Sakenfeld, with a feminist lens, notes that a "story with promising beginnings, as women seek to make their own way, ends very conventionally ... with the women's security achieved by reintegrating themselves completely into the existing traditional economic and family structures." She moves us to a congregational setting, asking, "How can such a story be read as a word that frees, as life-giving, as a text having authority, as a word of good news to readers who see so many human inadequacies in the presuppositions, the processes, and the end result of the narrative?"[14] Her questions are not dismissive of the text, but rather provoke renewed and critical assessment of our own cultural context.

Sensitivity to the kind of company you keep as a preacher—or the kind of company you would like to welcome—should act as a guide as you build your library.

---

11. Schipper, *Ruth*, 128.
12. Schipper, *Ruth*, 31.
13. Schipper, *Ruth*, 31.
14. Sakenfeld, *Ruth*, 86.

Part Two: Tinkering

Creature Comforts

When I wrote for an online commentary, a colleague who was writing for the same commentary groused: "Be careful. I think people are just cutting and pasting our commentary for their sermons." My colleague might have been disappointed in me but what I write for a commentary is generally pretty good and when I write for a commentary, I don't write *for* a commentary—I write for the human being who I know will be reading it and is probably run ragged with too many things to do. If I give that person an idea, something to run with, I say God bless them.

Homiletics caught the disease of originality from Western academics, where everything is copyrighted and the fight, the scrum, the backstabbing for an "original" thought is the gold fleece of academic life. If that's the way the academy chooses to regulate itself, that's fine. There are good arguments for that kind of self-regulation in academia. But preaching belongs to an ancient tradition, as ancient as the biblical stories themselves. Read the Bible and you're not reading, by and large, original material. It constantly recasts, revisits, recalls a first story, a myth that somehow reincarnates in every new setting—I find that useful, enriching, and liberating. I also think it belongs to a traditional understanding of knowledge, as an inheritance, not unlike Paul's, "for I have received from Jesus what I also pass on to you." Grift has nothing to do with it and gift everything to do with it. The debate about "originality" or "plagiarism" in preaching is a uniquely Western phenomenon.

Maybe a better alternative is found in Native traditions of storytelling. Mischa Willett retells the Raven story of the Tlingit:

> A long time ago, the raven looked down from the sky and saw that the people of the world were living in darkness. The ball of light was kept hidden by a selfish old chief. So the raven turned itself into a spruce needle and floated on the river where the chief's daughter came for water. She drank the spruce needle. She became pregnant and gave birth to a boy which was the raven in disguise. The baby cried and cried until the chief gave him the ball of light to play with. As soon as he had the light, the raven turned back into himself and carried the light into the sky. From then on, we no longer lived in darkness.[15]

---

15. Willett, "Shape-Shifter," 35.

Creature Comforts

This is one of first stories you hear as a child growing up in Alaska. When I told my daughter, Iris, the story of Raven, I told her a version that says that Raven escaped through the smoke hole of the chief's long house and that's why the Raven is black today. My daughter seemed pleased with that explanation.

Willett believes that there is a difference between the story of Scripture and the plasticity of Raven:

> [The Raven story] has traveled well beyond [the Pacific Northwest], wandering in and out of other stories like some curious bird. In poems, every word matters. In holy scripture, the Word is what matters. But here, though the language and idiom may change with time and taste, the cycle is what matters. Being myth, the raven story can change its contours with each telling, but so long as certain events take place, it remains raven cycle. It is itself, you might say, in whatever form it takes.[16]

Willet may be thinking of the tension between the Scripture as *verbo* or *sermo*: in the case of *verbo*, the word is complete, finished and in that sense, *logos* "matters" as an enclosed meaning without reference to other contextual elements. By contrast, in *sermo*, the word gains significance through conversation or weaving things together—without that openness it ceases to be. If one takes conversation as the basis of the Word, then it follows that the "cycle" of the Word may remain the same but the partners to that conversation weave together its meaning, or even open it up to the possibility of meaning.

The principle of translation, which is not far from *sermo*, which recasts a story in a new voice, in a new body, in a new place, "refreshes" the meaning or even make it new. Willett points to an example of Singletary's work, which had taken a story she knew by heart and made it new again:

> Where I had the "chief's daughter drank the spruce needle that was Raven in disguise" the text accompanying the show . . . reads "Yeil is ingested by Naas Shaak Aank-a'awu du Se'ek' and she becomes pregnant with Yeil," with all the proper names rendered in Tlingit. I still remember the first time I read the Bible in French. When I read about these guys following Jesus called "Pierre, Jean, and Jacques," I just couldn't get over it. The names sounded too contemporary, ridiculous even. Of course, I realize that no one in first century Nazareth was calling out "Gee-zuss" either, but on some linguistic level, I couldn't hear it at first, wrapped in that new idiom. And when I did,

---

16. Willett, "Shape-Shifter," 35.

my understanding of the Gospels changed. *The flannelgraph cutouts took on flesh, became as real as rocks.*[17]

The myth of Raven, and its being recast in different mediums (languages), acts as an antidote to Western notions of originality, or verbum. It is not new; the story has been refashioned in a different place or with a different context and conversation partners. Singletary enjoys recasting totems or hats from their traditional mediums of cedar to bronze or crystal. Yet the extravagance of Singletary's translational impulse poses a problem: "These translations challenge what, in effect, the thing actually *is*. What's a totem pole that isn't made of wood? What's a totem that can fit in one's hands? What if it isn't even columnar?"[18]

Some First Nations artists resist translatability while others find inspiration in the dynamic of familiar-unfamiliar. Missiologists understand the translation principle as something unique to Christian narratives—whereas Islam and Judaism rendered the original language as the divine language, the Christian narrative is not divine until it finds its voice in the heart language of the recipient.

What approach might make our "old" stories new? The authors of the *First Nations Version: An Indigenous Translation of the New Testament*, introduce their work as arising from a desire to connect "in a culturally relevant way, to the traditional heart-languages of the over six million English-speaking First Nations people of North America." To do so, they translated the New Testament in its "dynamic equivalent" for First Nations rather than a "word-for-word translation"[19]—however, the "thought-for-thought" description understates what they achieve, particularly as they aim for a contextually meaningful translation. Hearing Matthew's 5:3–11 in dynamic equivalency with First Nations heart language makes the familiar unfamiliar. A selection:

> Creator's blessing rests on the poor, the ones with broken spirits.
> The good road from above is theirs to walk.
> Creator's blessing rests on those who walk a trail of tears,
> for he will wipe the tears from their eyes and comfort them . . .
> Creator's blessing rests on the ones who are merciful and kind to others.
> Their kindness will find its way back to them—full circle.[20]

17. Willett, "Shape-Shifter," 36, my italics.
18. Willett, "Shape-Shifter," 40.
19. *First Nations Version*, xi–xii.
20. *First Nations Version*, 6.

Recasting these familiar words in the language of the "trail of tears" startles with its sudden and strange clarity and yet is familiar as an old voice speaking in the dark by a fire.

Singletary's art of shifting mediums and shapes creates a hybridity or a syncretistic art that is a regular part of dynamic mapping between worlds of Scripture and the worlds of the twenty-first century. Syncretistic qualities, honestly named, unlock root narratives in uniquely meaningful ways. "Mixing," according to Willett, "is a strength. Concrete was actually quite brittle until someone thought to add iron rebar." Singletary, as mixed blood (Tlingit and White), exists in that translational zone. "By casting the traditional in new mediums . . . believing that there's something in the old chief's cedar box worth *getting*, his work changes things, illuminating the spruce, the woman, the child, the chief, the sky."[21] It feels somewhat like the preacher who, at least symbolically, is mixed blood, adopted by Christ and born of a human being.

Signposts for the Footpath

What are some basic strategies for using commentary, especially in the desert? Imagine a not super-inspiring text or time of day—not difficult to do. Yet, if you've yoked yourself to a daily or weekly discipline, this will be one of your watering holes. Sometimes, you feel like the woman at Jacob's well—why do I have to keep coming to this well, week after week, and in the heat of the day, when everyone else has got on with their lives? What tips would I offer you?

A commentary is most useful somewhere between the first engaged reading of the text and the first draft (750 or so words). Either before or after those 750 words, write a clear theme statement, including a focus (theological action) and function (human need). Go to the hymns for the service. This is often overlooked between exegesis, creative reading, and so on—yet a good hymnal contains a rich and widely shared commentary that reflects the piety and poetry of Scripture and theological traditions. We won't bless all the

21. Willett, "Shape-Shifter," 43.

theology represented in a hymnal—you argue against some of those ideas, engage in a conversation with others, and find the prayer that is better than your sermonic point. Experiment with hymn selection before going to the biblical commentary. Your community will thank you because, first, it helps musicians who need more notice and, second, because it helps you hear how the church as a faith community has heard these texts and themes. It's almost as if the hymns give the color scheme, the pallet. It becomes a part of my "medium" so much so that I forget that I am swimming with different hues of blue or red or yellow. By the time Sunday comes, I'm happily surprised by the linkages between hymns, text, and sermon—they grew together while I slept!

When you open the commentary, don't demand relevance to the sermon idea. Practically, use the commentary after you have established a rapport with the text, including recognizing the text's oddities, some notion of its structure, what it might mean. Write this down, either as a condensed theme or as a twenty-five-word statement, "This text means . . ." Consult biblical commentary in the spirit that the sermon exists as a form of public intellectual activity—while the sermon may contain my personal signature it is not reduced to my personality as such. Over time, I have found that listeners are, at heart, curious about the Bible, what it means in its own setting, and how it can be meaningful for our setting. Listeners treat a sermon as a part of a pastoral relationship, in which they have entrusted their pastor with the vocation of interpretation. When we enter a conversation with biblical scholars, we do so not in place of local theology but on its behalf.

Remember: that gray, dull feeling that slips over you isn't unique to you. It happens to everyone and to the best of them. The difference between those who thrive as biblical interpreters and those who don't is that those who thrive treat each encounter as potentially rich. Keep a notepad at hand. When I'm tired, at the end of my reading session, I ask, "What are three to five things I learned from this encounter?" In so doing, I never leave an encounter empty-handed. The well may be deep, my bucket may be rusting out, and I may be fed up with coming here, but I know that, in a day or later that afternoon, if I look at my notes, I will see something that slaked my thirst or at least did so partially.

Read it, note it, leave it—resist the temptation of this exercise providing a "jack-in-the-box" kind of moment. Spend twenty or thirty minutes of reading and noting . . . or fifteen minutes. Then leave it. Demand nothing of yourself or it. Go do something else. Knock about. Do some yoga stretches.

Generally, do whatever looks like goofing off compared to being hunched over a thick volume, going blind with concentration. Live.

When I read published works, I think a couple of things: first, it is in print, second, it comes with a seal of a respected publishing house; so mostly I read in a deferential spirit. I put my agenda on hold as I entertain the insights won by exhaustive scholarship. I also read as one who knows the "publish or perish" mentality, and I know that academics suffer from the same human frailties as the rest of us. The institutional trappings of theological education sometimes ask that their members publish not because they feel that calling but because it views publications as a marketing tool, increasing its commercial value. With that in mind, sometimes you will look at something in print, nice binding, respected publishing house, but you find in it straw, and straw, and more straw. Pray for the person who wrote it because they are captive to a commercial imperative rather than a vocation of scholarship.

When I think about "bring my cloak," I think of acceptance of myself, my gifts and abilities as they are, as a preacher that what I have to offer on a given Sunday is an acceptable offering if it is given in humility and love. I may not be fully "texted" up—may not be fully acquainted with the map of the text, in other words, the commentary on the text, but I accept that God equips us all with something that may help others in that Sunday morning hour. It may be rambling, but it is, one hopes, a loving ramble. I begin to see what is in my life, on the walk path, or just off from it. As I think about the text, I think about what is nearest to me, if it is the fields, then it is the fields; if it is the streets, then it is the streets; if it is near, it bears witness and I listen for its word because it comes to me in a place of readiness, openness. It is not scripted the way a sermon is scripted, or the way the text is scripted, or the way a commentary is scripted, but in the way of all that is . . . the wind blows where it wills, all are born of the Spirit.

It is possible to say, "I got it wrong" in my initial hunch—it is also possible to resist the claim of the text (and the biblical commentary) and do so with a form of human dignity that I think Jesus would approve. I am thinking of a sermon about forgiveness on Matthew 18:21–22, when Jesus says, forgive seventy times seven. It was preached around the time of George Floyd's death. I could not go with the text, at least not directly. In the end, I spoke of this curious fascination with numbers, not only the numerology of our Judeo-Christian tradition, but the "numerology" of our own day, how many minutes the police officer kept his knee on Floyd's neck, how many

Part Two: Tinkering

times he cried for his mother. Perhaps the call to forgive comes too cheaply, too quickly especially with White communities.

Was this in a commentary? No. But the commentary wasn't the real burden that the congregation was called to carry that day.

Chapter Five

Wooden Tongue

"[The person learning to walk with a prosthetic must relearn] that childhood thing of not falling over, developing muscle strength, but all without the feedback of healthy skin touching the floor or the side of the shoe."

—Graham B. Usher, *The Way Under Our Feet*

On a run through Baltimore's Druid Hill Park, I felt a strain in my right hip. I didn't think much of it at the time; I kept running. And then, as often happens on a run, my loop kept getting bigger, so that eventually a three-mile turned into a seven-mile circuit through rolling hills. I also felt a moment of my former self, the younger version of myself as I ran, the twenty-something who still viewed everything as competition. The twenty-something urged my fifty-something on, ignoring the pain—and then I got home. I knew something was wrong when, after showering, I nearly toppled over because I had no strength at all in my right hip.

Give it a couple of weeks, I thought. It began to feel better. And I started to run again, just a couple of miles, nothing too demanding. Pain still lurked in the background, but it wasn't stopping me. Then upheaval in our lives as I prepared to leave my pastorate in Baltimore to try a new life in England, where my wife's family lives. Our family of six landed at

Part Two: Tinkering

Manchester International on December 8, 2020, the entirety of our material lives distilled down to six large suitcases.

We arrived just before lockdown. We were in quarantine and leaving the house wasn't an option, so I jogged in circles in a boggy part of the garden. As soon as we were out of quarantine, I launched myself on a run that kept going, first up the lane, then left down the side of Annel Cross Moor, right onto a bridle path skirting the edge of the Upper and Lower Black Moss Reservoirs, into the village of Barley, up the Pendle footpath, finally to the trig point at 557 meters, the highest part of the peak, and down again to our cottage in Twiston . . . and perhaps you see where this is going. The injury grew more difficult to ignore, impacting not only my ability to run, but to walk. Soon, for the first time in my life, I could barely walk up the lane without excruciating pain. I was downing maximum doses of Ibuprofen, soaking in a hot bath, being as gentle with myself as I knew how, but nothing seemed to ease the pain.

Then one day my father-in-law came back from one of his walks with the LADS, a small group of men who have been walking together for years. Grinning broadly, he presented me with a new gift: a walking stick with a handle topped off with a deer's antler. I took it, though not with any great joy. It felt like I'd been sentenced, not only by the revolt in my hip but by the judgment of others who had seen me hobbling around and finally concluded I needed some assistance. When I told my new employer of my injury, they asked, "Do I need to know anything?"—in that self-important tone of voice that some managers use to inform you that they see you as a potential liability to the organization.

Altogether, that injury plagued me for nearly eight months, probably extended by my stubborn determination to "pretend" everything was just fine. After a strong prescription of painkillers and a few visits to an orthopedic physician who specializes in sports injuries, I was feeling more myself. I haven't quite forgotten that injury. My fifty-four-year-old body views the enthusiasms of my twenty-two-year-old self with a different, more sober eye. But that brief stint with minor physical disability and the prospect of a walking stick—at one point the worry that I would never be able to roam the hills again, much less run, led me nearly to despair—gave me a tiny glimpse of what it means to experience a diminishment of the physical abilities that the able-bodied mostly take for granted.

A Wooden Identity

Why do I share this? Because no matter how prepared I am or even unprepared, the sermon feels wooden, and so does the identity of being a preacher. Is it a sort of prosthetic? It seems odd to think like this but the whole idea of being a "preacher" feels wooden. Instead of resisting or arguing with it, maybe we live with that feeling. If we do live with that idea, it may feel like the most horrible prosthetic you can imagine—wood, bolts, and bindings. And yet, it happens that we experience ourselves as preachers, maybe even with a message of beauty, or we are seen as preachers whether we see ourselves that way or not. We undergo something, an amputation, and an extension.

This feels like a profound kind of question and something that has unclear boundaries. I'm choosing to ground this chapter in something tangible and yet also potentially evocative, namely the manuscript. We might experience some shame in being a "manuscript preacher"—my preaching teacher once said that the best sermons are often written, but the most beautiful and inspired sermons are completely oral. Early in ministry, I would spend Fridays and often a Saturday night (I led a lonely life) committing a written sermon to memory, so that my tongue would move as effortlessly as the wind.

Another highly regarded homiletician and preacher advises that we should go through our manuscript seven times, out loud, to achieve the level of oral-aural immediacy in the preaching moment. I outdid that recommendation, recording each effort and playing back while under the dim lights of the sanctuary, editing and changing things as I went along. As a teacher, I modified this approach, but not by much. Perhaps not surprisingly, some of my former students came back after a few years in the pulpit and said they had given up the manuscript. They claimed their congregations loved the difference it made. Maybe it was like a scene from the movie *Forrest Gump*, with the group of boys chasing him, his legs moving clumsily and slowly in his leg braces. Eventually, Forrest's braces begin to disintegrate, bolts and screws popping out, bands of steel and leather straps falling away from his running legs. That's the story anyway—and despite my love of that movie, it doesn't ring true.

I can't memorize sermons anymore. It just doesn't work, not with my memory. Plus, I'm not as lonely on a Saturday night as I once was—kids and marriage will do that for a person. But my commitment to manuscript is not all deficiency: "My tongue is like the pen of a ready scribe" sings the

Part Two: Tinkering

psalmist (Ps 45:1); Paul asks that his *letters* be read out loud in the congregation (Col 4:16); and reading the Beatitudes of Matthew 5:1–11 in the silence of one's own mind cannot do justice to the auralization of these words, as the tongue rescues the sound of these beautiful words from the text for our listening community, which feels anew the ache and stately dignity of Jesus' Sermon on the Mount. Somehow, the leg braces of manuscript do not only "correct" a deficiency—in ways that I don't fully understand, the words on a page, powerless in their two-dimensionality, loosen the tongue until it becomes like a wing, spontaneous in love and feeling and, at other times, as stately and poised as a marriage vow.

We don't do a good job with this tension, between the prosthetic limb for the tongue (the manuscript) and the voice of the preacher. If they do exist together, it is an uneasy relationship—in some cases, it feels as if the manuscript is, indeed, the enemy of the oral-aural moment of preaching. And yet . . .

On the one hand, I am curious about my ambivalence to the presence of paper in the preaching moment. I prefer not to see it even if I understand that it is present in the speaking moment. I would like it to almost disappear completely. The last thing I want is to listen to or be experienced by a listener as a "manuscript preacher"—a thing that feels somehow disparaging, like being called a "cripple" by "ableists" who claim to speak without a manuscript. On the other hand, with no manuscript, we lose an opportunity for something more than friendly rambling. We think of the word as mysterious and majestic and the human voice as the "elect" member for that expression (Rom 10:14–15).

Why is this chapter important to those who may share this ambivalence towards the manuscript? Four reasons: (1) Because so many people reject the manuscript as if it were second-class to the "natural" voice in extempore mode; (2) because so many people become "manuscript preachers"—their mode of communicating being the most notable (and tragic) characteristic of their preaching; (3) for those who feel as if the manuscript is, potentially, their tongue, we can learn the prosthetic until it becomes our freely chosen tongue, a stick of wood that sings, of which we may be proud; (4) it is not only the preacher who learns to use the wooden tongue but the congregation that acquires a capacity to hear its music—those who live with sermons include not only those who write and preach sermons but also those who listen for the Word of God in the very human sermon.

Prosthetic: A Deficiency

Paul's rhetorical question in Romans 10:14–15 comes to mind: "But how are they to call on one in whom they have not believed? And how are they to believe in one of whom they have never heard? And how are they to hear without someone to proclaim him? And how are they to proclaim unless they are sent? As it is written, 'How beautiful are the feet of those who bring good news!'"

Salvation enters the heart by way of the ear that has, in the psalmist's language, been "dug" or carved out of hard-of-hearing stone (Ps 40:6). Instead of an open ear, it invades a sealed tomb; instead of a tongue, a stick of wood? Could it be that the paper opposes, imprisons, reduces, takes human voice as its most prized captive, turns the human tongue into a robot that simply repeats its phrases and marks? Maybe that's why Annie Dillard spoke to me when she answers the question, "Who will teach me to write?" The teacher, she says, is the page. But it feels almost like being introduced to the enemy of expression or its radical amputation: "the page . . . the page of your death . . . that page will teach you to write."[1]

Rethink the manuscript: it is not the "friend" of those who preach. It is among our deadliest enemies—or paradoxically one of our most powerful allies. Yet it feels alien to the tongue, even more so than to the writer. The Chilean poet Pablo Neruda gives this a memorable twist with his poem, "A Foot to Its Child": "A child's foot is not yet aware it is a foot, and would like to be a butterfly or an apple."[2] How will we approach the manuscript? Or is the manuscript trying to tell us that it is our tongue, as we try to use it incorrectly as a foot?

In sucking on our toes, we detect the indirect art of learning our foot, learning our voice from a page.

The sermon makes impossible demands on the mind and tongue—is the manuscript the prosthetic tongue of the preacher? Or how not? Paul Ricoeur teaches us that in every metaphor we find an "is" and an "is not"— an alive metaphor shows or declares something true and not true at the same time. So, if we say, the manuscript is a tongue, we may instinctively react to that assertion, NO! On the other hand, those who live with sermons experience the written page as an almost natural extension of their tongue, perhaps an even "better" tongue than the one they were born with. So, is

---

1. Dillard, *Writing Life*, 58–59.
2. Neruda, *Extravagaria*, 103.

Part Two: Tinkering

the manuscript a symbol of a deficiency? Or a replacement? An extension? Or could a prosthetic tongue be viewed as a medium for people who live with "mixed abilities"? A support group for disabled persons in Manchester chose that term, "mixed abilities" over "disabilities," as more representative of their experience. It is a useful way of thinking about the prosthetic of the tongue, the written word, a mixed ability. This chapter reflects on the phenomenon of the manuscript as a prosthetic for the voice or, alternatively, as mixed media for the person who lives with preaching. It may be possible that we come to inhabit that prosthetic so completely that it becomes indistinguishable from the voice/body of the person who preaches.

When we think of the prosthetic, we may think of the artificial limb. The word's meaning has evolved over time. Its Latin combines two words, *pro* (forward) + *thesis*, denoting an addition or extension. Historically, a prosthesis was used in grammar to refer to the addition of a syllable or letter at the beginning of a word. Later, in the sixteenth century, it became a figurative term for a surgical prosthesis. *The Oxford English Dictionary* defines prosthetics as "the branch of surgery concerned with the replacement of defective or absent parts of the body by artificial substitutes".[3]

Paint may not only signify a lack but also give shape to something within the artist. Artists work with limited mediums for the communication or conveyance of things that are just beyond the limit of human language. Something similar could be said of the preacher and the manuscript, or the words on a page. Does the laborious act of writing, of sounding out, of testing and striking out bring something together, something that we did not imagine and would not create were we simply "free" with our words? The preacher stands among poets, or at least as a minor poet, according to Craig Barnes, recent president of Princeton Theological Seminary. A poet not only writes poetically but the poem teaches the poet how to write. And so, in this way, thinking of the manuscript as a prosthetic for the tongue gives us a different way of viewing the preaching moment, or perhaps a new word for our tongue.

Maybe this is why artists show up so often in works about preaching. We live with the mixed abilities of our mediums. Dillard tells the story of a university student who asked a well-known writer whether he could be a writer. The writer asked him, "Do you like sentences?" This seemed a ludicrous sort of question to ask a twenty-year-old aspiring to greatness. But it brought to Dillard's mind a painter she knew: "I asked him how he came

---

3. Coffey, "Prosthesis."

to be a painter. He said, 'I liked the smell of paint.'"[4] Each year, students would come to my office and tell me that preaching was their great passion. I didn't know what to tell them. I wish I had said, "Do you like the sound of words? Do you like playing with them, seeing or hearing what they evoke? Learn words! Sleep with a thesaurus. Let the memory of Scripture resuscitate empty lungs."

Most people who want to be great preachers simply want to be great. Preaching is simply the sideshow. Sometimes they do go on to enjoy greatness. But not because of their preaching.

In his book *The Way Under Our Feet*, Graham B. Usher relates the observation of an orthopedic surgeon who works with former military personnel who lost limbs in Afghanistan and Iraq. He relates how people living with amputated limbs would begin their journey or physical rehab courageously and then, about three months in, they would realize that the loss of a limb is permanent, and it will not be growing back. Even with the advances in prosthetic limbs, the challenge of learning to walk with a prosthetic remains: "[The person learning to walk with a prosthetic must relearn] that childhood thing of not falling over, developing muscle strength, but all without the feedback of healthy skin touching the floor or the side of the shoe."[5]

As people write for preaching, they may feel that numbness, that absence of "healthy skin" in touch with the shoe or floor. You feel numb, or what you felt in its inarticulate form becomes loutish in its written form. Maybe the best we can do is to prepare ourselves for disappointment: "[our writing on the page] is not the vision filled in, as if it had been a coloring book. . . . It is rather a simulacrum and a replacement. It is a golem. You try—you try every time—to reproduce the vision, to let your light so shine before men. But you can only come along with your bushel and hide it."[6]

How, then, to use this page, this wooden tongue—can it be anything other than golem, a wooden replacement for the tongue?

Learning Our Wooden Tongue

There is something that happens when you sit down to write a sermon. What seemed almost at your fingertips withdraws, like one of those dreams

---

4. Dillard, *Writing Life*, 70.
5. Usher, *Way Under Our Feet*, 31.
6. Dillard, *Writing Life*, 58.

of delicious food, fruit, and meat, that as you reach to take, its satisfaction vanishes. This is the experience of having an idea or more gloriously a vision and sitting down to write it on to a page of paper. The beginning is the most hateful of all. You must pray. Then write. And write: "You write it all, discovering it at the end of the line of words. The line of words is a fiber optic, flexible as wire; it illumines the path just before its fragile tip. You probe with it, delicate as a worm."[7] We discover "it" at the end of a line of words. The tongue lives through words and sentences like a worm.

"Few sights are so absurd as that of an inchworm leading its dimwit life"—this is the inauspicious introduction of the writer's life, and perhaps the life of the person who lives with sermons. "Every inchworm I have seen was stuck in long grasses. The wretched inchworm hangs from the side of a grassblade and throws its head around from side to side, seeming to wail. What! No further? . . . Every step brings it to the universe's rim. And now—What! No further? Yike! 'Why don't you just jump?' I tell it, disgusted. 'Put yourself out of your misery.'"[8]

Replace the word inchworm with "preacher"—is it any wonder that we dread writing? It feels like an impossibility. I pour myself into a scriptural world, feel as if I'm living in it, I hear my voice giving expression to that world extempore in a moment of proclamation only witnessed by the world God so loves—the sheep of the field, and the wolf-caterpillar, the Curlew haunting my path in circles of seeming curiosity—yet as soon as I put a word on paper, I'm almost sorry about it. The person who lives with sermons gets a little perch on this grass blade and maybe for a moment thinks I've got something, but it doesn't last, soon we feel as if we are flailing about in space, desperate for a thesaurus, a Google search, a text from someone that will rescue us from drowning. And then it happens, and it feels like dumb luck, but you find a word, and then another, and another—in between panic attacks—an unlikely analogy, a story you hadn't thought about

---

7. Dillard, *Writing Life*, 7.
8. Dillard, *Writing Life*, 7–8.

in ages, and at the end, you say, "There's something!" It may be only fleeting but it is enough, it is the ephemeral that hints at the beautiful.

What do you do when the sermon idea you had turns to nothing? It was clear but then something happened . . . it began to collapse on itself. It is not that you expect your sermon on a page to be fire. You can't continue with it. It is too ugly, too sick. Dillard admits that she doesn't write a book as much as she "sit[s] up with it, as with a dying friend."[9] And yet, sometimes we're surprised, delighted when we come back the next day—you might see something if you return to it later. Similarly, as we live with a sermon: it feels like something we do out of tenderness and in the faint hope that, despite all the troubles we see in our work, it might just get better. You don't know, sometimes when you leave the hospital room, you think, "Not much longer." And yet, sometimes we're surprised, delighted when we come back the next day—you might see something if you return to it later.

We will return to it. Sunday's coming and we can only pretend it's not coming for so long. Give yourself a break from its groans. Visit this thing in another place, in a park, or near the sounds of other people's work or play. Starting again is the norm, not the exception. The line of words finds its goal as you move from left to right. On the first page, it feels like the path. Uninteresting but reliable. Then something happens. Your mind wanders. You find yourself in a different place, but you don't yet know its difference. This difference, something natural that just came up, may become the lens by which you see everything else, the slanted way of a metaphor that captures the light of the text.

Dillard operates with the writer's rhythm, which is not measured by the Sabbath. But anyone who lives with the sermon as a thing that changes or evolves or becomes terribly ill, recognizes the pattern. You write. You wait a day or an afternoon or perhaps a week or two if you plan further out. You visit it again. It looks like something may be good. But it is also very sick. We do not "preach sermons" so much as we linger with them, gently, prayerfully. We're not like a family member who cannot imagine their beloved succumbing to disease. We know. Works stronger than this have failed. Yet we also know that sometimes the patient gets better. Sometimes the patient tells us something, either by the way they respond or their gait or their description of pain, so hostile to language, but it provides a hint. We change our approach. Its path to wellness is not the path that we began, but somewhere else.

9. Dillard, *Writing Life*, 52.

Part Two: Tinkering

"You may wonder how to start . . ." Perhaps we should remind ourselves that where we start is seldom our start. Where we start is often more excuse or just flailing—or the dull thud of wood on dirt. But the writing hand moves and if we desire its insight, we follow it. "What," Dillard asks, "do you use for bait?" That is, how do you "catch" your beginning, your flame that will continue to burn in this sermon? She tells the story of an Algonquin woman and her baby, the lone survivors after everyone else in their camp had starved. The woman found a small stash of fishing things, a line and hook, but no bait. For bait, "she took a knife and cut a strip from her own thigh. She fished with the worm of her own flesh and caught a jackfish; she fed the child and herself."[10] From the fish, she used its gut for bait and, in the spring, returned to her people. She carried the scar on her thigh.

Sometimes I hear preachers talk about "the hook"—that's how they claim to start their sermons. I suppose it means the human connection, the need we care about, but it's a bad choice of words. Better you begin with the "worm of your own flesh"—the line, the hook, they will only be instruments. But your flesh, the worm of it, gets my interest, my hunger, my anger. You will not catch many fish with a hook. But you must find the worm of flesh—for this thing we only have words, a knife for our flesh.

Work from word to word. Exert precision in your choice of language. Dillard describes this as the way a cell forms, one cell splitting into another and then another and so on until a body of work appears. It can be tedious. On the other side: do not interfere with the words as they come. Just keep writing. Or do not stop walking. Carry on. It is not important that everything you say follows a clear line. Leave it. Let it grow, fold, collapse, turn, disappear, resurface, scuttle, dart, and stand still. You stop eventually (we all stop) and then later you come back to the words, sentences. You feel that you have something to work with—neither wholly beautiful nor altogether disappointing. It feeds you, the person who lives with sermons, to cast your line again. You caught something.

Sermons are wooden things, uncomfortable to those who live with them as well as for those who listen to them. This has led some to say that the sermon must go—or that the sermon is overrated. Of course it's overrated. It's the Word of God. But here's a reason to carry on with this prosthetic tongue—precisely because it lacks obvious power. Every generation promotes something better than a wooden sermon. Once it was the cult of

---

10. Dillard, *Writing Life*, 12–13.

Wooden Tongue

personality; now maybe we flock to the Ted Talk video. Dillard finds in the lives of insects delightfully horrifying—and to that extent truthful—analogies for our own behavior: a study of the male butterfly shows that it will ignore the real, living female butterfly in favor of a large, painted cardboard representation of a female butterfly. "Why," asks Dillard, "would anyone read a book instead of watching big people move on a screen?"[11]

We hear a variation on this question asked about the sermon. People, we are told, don't want sermons. They don't listen to monologues. Or they prefer commercials, Twitter, TikTok, and so on—let's turn the sermon into a TikTok. It will be better that way, as "bigger" media. Dillard understands the difference between the "bigger" media and the "wooden" media of a book—a sermon, like a book, cannot compete with a TikTok. It shouldn't try not only because there's no competition (TikTok wins every time) but because they are different things. Books do something that only books can do or perhaps they do something for people who prefer books.[12] Can we imagine a community where people prefer sermons? Someone probably wants to laugh, as in a joke. But this is no joke: Do we know anyone who looks forward to the sermon on Sunday? Or people who choose to live with sermons as a basic condition of their communion with God? A 2016 Pew Research study surveyed five thousand people asking them to list the top reasons for choosing their church home. More than eight out of ten (83 percent) listed quality preaching as their top concern.[13] Most people listen, apparently closely, to the sermon. Some people prefer this thing we call a sermon. They have an idea of what they're listening for, rather like people who read books have an idea of why they read. Why preach at all for people who do not want something called a sermon? "I cannot imagine a sorrier pursuit," says Dillard, "than struggling for years to write a book that attempts to appeal to people who do not read in the first place."[14]

But this wooden thing. A sermon. You cannot treat it as if it were wholly alien or entirely natural. It resuscitates collapsed lungs; it palpitates arrested hearts. The living thing for which we search, word to flailing word, the worm of flesh which first catches us, the word that palpitates and breathes—it first enters us, the preacher:

---

11. Dillard, *Writing Life*, 18.
12. Dillard, *Writing Life*, 19.
13. Pew Research Center, "Choosing a New Church or House of Worship."
14. Dillard, *Writing Life*, 19.

Part Two: Tinkering

> The [sermon] must enter the body, too. A [preacher] cannot use [sermons] like glue or screws to fasten down the world. [Sermons] are like fingers; they work only if, inside the [preacher], the neural pathways are wide and clear to the brain. Cell by cell, molecule by molecule, atom by atom, part of the brain changes physical shape to accommodate and fit [the sermon].[15]

If you want to write, you need to love words, sentences. You need to smell the paint, enjoy it, the promise of a blank page. Sleep with a thesaurus. But to preach, you also need to love the physical expression of those words. Enjoy the physical action of the word as it blossoms in the warmth of a voice or in changes of pitch between interrogation of a text and the formation of our souls. You don't need to become a rhetorician. You simply need a better rhetoric. My mother tells me that as she works with clay, she listens for its shape. She responds to that felt shape even as she shapes. Maybe what we need is the rhetoric that enters you or that you hear speaking in the clay of a text or idea.

After an hour or two (or years) of writing sermons we recognize Dillard's revelation about her own experience as a writer: "The writing has changed, in your hands, and in a twinkling, from an expression of your notions to an epistemological tool. The new place interests you because it is not clear. You attend."[16] I only discover what is interesting and what is not clear—and therefore inviting—after I have disposed of a path that wasn't going anywhere. I took a path with a particular intention. I follow it, not with any great insight. It usually feels stale. But I have to say something, don't I? So, I write. It feels like an excuse. But I don't know how else to get to that place where I am attending in some way to a clue or a question that feels like a living thing. Dillard compares the creative work of a painter with that of a writer. The painter, she says, covers her tracks: "The latest version of the painting overlays earlier versions, and obliterates them. Writers, on the other hand, work from left to right."[17] The stuff on your left, she says, feels "lumpish" and the work's real beginning greets the reader on the right, on the wrong hand. This is why preaching feels like an upside-down world—or a backwards world.

Fran Auerbach confirms Dillard's intuition about painters: he painted the same North London streets for over sixty years. In a letter written to the Glasgow Museum that houses his work, he explained:

15. Dillard, *Writing Life*, 69.
16. Dillard, *Writing Life*, 3.
17. Dillard, *Writing Life*, 5.

> Mornington Crescent Winter Morning 1989 was certainly done from many quick sketches made at a site near me—there would have been over a hundred of them—repainted every day from the added impressions recorded in the sketches, over a long period of time. It would have changed with the seasons—Winter refers to the time it was finished.[18]

For those who live in the preacher's studio, most sermons are not as "finished" as they may feel in the moment. And perhaps they never will be. This is what we mean when we say that most preachers have only two or three sermons, which they preach for their whole lives. But it's a message viewed at dusk or in the light of a busy afternoon or with eyes still sick from fever. You don't get to "finished"—instead, the world looks on and sees what you have done, doesn't necessarily get the restlessness with which you treat your theme. Maybe some do. But this isn't about them, at least not yet. For the time being, it is about you, you as you scrape away the paint, adjust the color scheme, discover a different way than the one you began. It is about the process of self-critique, or maybe the discovery of the better word, or simply the relatively adequate word. And we say, "It's finished"—until it begins again.

The Self-Edit

The irony of the sermon as an event is that it feels as if it were born in that very moment, flesh and blood, word on the lips and tongue. We think, "It dropped from God, into my head, and rolled out my mouth. Amen." Maybe in the theological world that's what happens, but in our world it is also the product of countless revisions, false starts, and scratching out. When a volume of T. S. Eliot's "The Waste Land" was printed, with notes from Ezra Pound and comments in the margins, strike-throughs, scribbles—it was almost a revelation to me. Eliot's poetry never fails to deliver subtle elegance, almost like an ancient liturgy. And yet, there on the page, were photos of this thing that seemed to have been worked over and crossed out, debated, and quibbled over. This word or that word? Can't decide. I was stunned. Here I was seeing the creative work, or its residue, like the place where lightning struck. Not long ago, the handwritten notes of Freddy Mercury revealed the beginning of Queen's classic "Bohemian Rhapsody." Mercury's handwritten notes scrawl across the page, "Nothing Really Matters to me"

---

18. Auerbach, "Letter to Glasgow Museum."

and then more lyrics on a defunct scheduling document for British Midland Airways. Some of what he wrote did not get much further than the scrap of paper it was written on—and some we now know by heart.

What I notice among skilled communicators and artists is an ability to get distance from the work at hand—that what we see in publication or hear on Sunday morning is only half the story. Artists grow and respond to the work being formed in them. I call the sermon the belly button of the person who preaches. It feels close and it is close. How do we get distance on that thing? Back in seminary, we got that kind of perspective in preaching labs. Two or three students would preach their sermons and receive "feedback" or "critique." We asked, what worked? What needs reworking? It was always the most difficult for the preacher, who fell somewhere between being either overly apologetic or fiercely protective of their work. As a teacher, I knew that what we were doing was important, namely the ability to think critically and constructively about our work, but the sermon critique was limited in its long-term usefulness.

We don't need a homiletical critique, at least not when we live with the sermon as a basic condition of our vocation. Instead, we need perspective. Susan Bell, a writer who thinks about the role of the edit, admits what we know to be true for creative types everywhere, and for preachers, too: "It is fair to say all writers—seasoned or not, steady or panicked—lose perspective."[19] According to Bell, getting distance from our work involves both a metaphysical and a physical challenge. The metaphysical and the physical are more closely related than we might imagine. Some of the more obvious physical practices:

- Change the font of the manuscript;
- Edit your sermon in a place other than where you wrote it;
- Use the "hang out" or "lay out" method—hang your manuscript from a clothes line or spread it out on the floor in your living room, preferably out of order;
- If you normally type, write in longhand and if using a computer, resist the delete and scroll back.[20]

These seem like small changes, but each change introduces a form of distance between how you imagine your work and the work itself.

19. Bell, *Artful Edit*, 12.
20. Bell, *Artful Edit*, 34.

Wooden Tongue

Go for practices that entangle the metaphysical with the physical. Read or wander through your sermon in an unusual setting (a homeless shelter, or at a protest or strike, or perhaps in the lobby of an expensive hotel, at a graveyard, or in a nursing home). These sorts of highly charged spaces are almost like the "thin places" of Celtic spirituality—you begin to see your work in a different light.

Other strategies make the sermon creation process more dialogical, a common expression among preachers. Key to Bell's conception, however, is that the preacher relinquishes her or his ego. To that end, let someone else read your sermon or, better yet, have someone read your sermon aloud, preferably someone who looks on the world through a different set of eyes than your own (life experience, gender, sexuality, age, ethnicity). Often, we cannot hear what we sound like until someone else speaks our words for us. A variation on this theme: read your sermon to a conversation partner, stopping from time to time to dialogue about the message.[21] Resist the temptation to "explain" your work; attend to what they heard, not what you meant. The metaphysical challenge goes to our own connection to the sermon, the sermon being something like the belly button of our soul. However, if we give the sermon up, release it to someone else, another listener or conversation partner, we can begin to hear it and a congregation's potential response more richly.

While in general friendly, prayerful editors help the preacher, it may not be altogether bad for us to cultivate a more critical congregation as well. Poet W. H. Auden speaks of developing his own "Inner Censorate," a group of imagined and not always sympathetic listeners: "a sensitive child, a practical housewife, a logician, a monk, an irreverent buffoon and even, perhaps . . . a foul mouthed drill sergeant who considers all poetry [sermons] rubbish."[22]

Bell asks us to exercise care at this moment: "Beware of the temptation to pander. If your Censorate overtakes you, stop listening to it altogether."[23] In other words, we need to be sufficiently confident in our interpretation of the text and the claim of the sermon to enter into a meaningful conversation. This is different than saying the sermon is six feet above contradiction;

---

21. Bell, *Artful Edit*, 27–28.
22. Bell, *Artful Edit*, 26–27.
23. Bell, *Artful Edit*, 27.

it means that the sermonic idea is mature, maybe not quite ready to be plucked from the tree but glowing with potentiality.[24]

Signposts for the Footpath

As people are being fitted with a prosthetic, they choose what works for them—and freely and imperiously reject what doesn't. That may be the most important thing that needs to be said here, especially if you were "fitted" with a prosthetic in seminary that didn't work for you or didn't work as well as you would like in some situations. We have natural preferences and maybe sometimes a situation leads us to choose something different. Sometimes the situation helps us decide which kind of prosthetic we will use, to fit the topic or occasion. If the sermon touches on a controversial or difficult topic, you may want to be exceptionally precise in your choice of words. Or if you find that you're exploring unfamiliar theological territory, the act of writing slows down the process, so you can attend to the topic. Sometimes the act of writing itself will raise the question of a fresh perspective. Or perhaps the sermon includes an object that, in a way, speaks. Whatever the object, it prompts your speaking.

It's best for a preacher to acquire a bevy of prosthetic tongues, maybe using more than one, a mix: a manuscript might include a personal narrative that you can tell from memory; or an object lesson; or moving to a different space in the sanctuary, creating a "scene" that helps you and the listener connect at a different place. Prosthetics may include full manuscripts, "mind maps" or familiarity with a well-formed "concept," or even the "tongue" of physical objects—each supply us with a means of extending the tongue or repairing an absence. As we learn to inhabit the prosthetic, we find our inner voice, the voice gifted to us by the Spirit, awakening on our tongues.

Even though you will have your favorites, it is good practice to gain familiarity with different styles, so that you come to enjoy the benefits of a mixed quiver of skills. As you probably know, a manuscript is often my preferred prosthetic, and my signposts go to that mode. How do I inhabit that

24. Hoch, "Gaining Perspective."

so that my inner voice, rather than the manuscript, is the thing that people hear? For one, I don't write in silence what I intend to speak out loud. When composing at a high level of anticipation (meaning, I am testing whether this is, in fact, where my tongue will be in the preaching moment), I speak the words as I write. Before, as I am searching, I often write in silence. But when I anticipate the oral-aural experience, I shift, often without knowing it (unless I am overheard by someone in the public library). Speaking then, rather than writing, is the object or goal or living memory represented by the ink marks on a page. When I look at the words on a page, I don't think of words so much as the sound of the word and its meaning in the sound.

As for the manuscript, use large font (sixteen- or eighteen-point type is easy to see and sometimes, if necessary, to read), use only the upper one-third of the page (keeps your gaze nearer to level with the congregation and reduces the "head-bobbing" associated with "manuscript preaching"). Sometimes I will highlight the first sentence, which functions as a cue for the movement. Think about how the words sound to the ear and use the manuscript to "signify" that sound. Paragraphs, like the one you're reading now, are for the reading eye—and perhaps the reading eye with reading glasses! The following is for the tongue and for the ear that would receive its testimony:

> A woman in her late thirties
>   says her mum is in the advanced stages of Alzheimer's.
>   She says that it wasn't the relationship she imagined
>   with her mum at this stage of life.
>   Her mum comes out of the shower,
>   she's forgotten to rinse the shampoo out of her hair.
>   She helps her back into the shower,
>   helps to rinse her hair.
> Her mother can't read anymore,
>   the words on the page make no sense,
>   but her three-year-old daughter
>   sits beside her,
>   pretend reading to grandma.
> It wasn't how
>   she expected it,
>   not how she imagined it,
>   and she wouldn't choose it,
>   a mum with dementia,
>   a mum . . .

Part Two: Tinkering

>   but somehow, she has found the strength to say,
>   thank you,
>   for this life,
>   for this love,
>   this love that lives even though we die.

The breaks remind you to linger with some words, or feel the pattern as it drops low, step by step to a dénouement, "this love that lives even though we die."

Use only one side of the page. You can keep two pages in front of you and never "turn" a page. Turning pages introduces inadvertent "visual" noise to the sermon. Using one side of the page does make for long sermon manuscripts. In the interest of being green, reuse the old manuscript but slash out the previous sermon to reduce risk of confusion.

Use your body to add "highlighter" to specific ideas. For example, if you want to amplify a series of traits or attributes, numbering three or four, use your hand to count out each attribute. The gesture acts as a metaphorical highlighter, setting it apart in a visual way, even as you're using a manuscript. This really extends to the whole physical space of the church. I'm not speaking about nervous wandering but intentional exploitation of the physical space for communication. What, for instance, would it be like to preach from the narthex, as you speak of the difference between being a "friendly" church and a "welcoming" church?

What about quotes? Manuscripts are dangerous this way—they can take over the preacher because they can hold many, many, many words, and many quotes by many worthies. Some sermons consist of one worthy quote after another before they finally wheeze out of existence with a footnote. At their best, quotes add diversity to the voice that you bring to the sermon. Very occasionally, a quote might be longer, particularly if it is a voice of someone that speaks out of an experience that the majority may not fully appreciate or may need to hear in its textured grittiness. Otherwise, quotes should be short, pithy, and memorable—and used sparingly, light salt, just enough to draw out the flavor of your topic.

As for memory, it may be useful for you to engage in this little exercise: take one page of your sermon and turn it face down. Try to speak it without looking at it. If you can't speak it, ask yourself, why? What did you remember? What did you forget? And then ask yourself, how necessary was it? If it was necessary, would an image or object or perhaps a physical location in the church give it the body and expression it deserves? If you're talking about shame, experiment with exchanging words for physical embodiment: if you're wearing an article of clothing, perhaps pull it over your face, to give a brief but memorable taste of the feeling of shame. In other words, it may be that what you've written is too much prose—straight prose is hard to remember, even if it is important. But a story, or an image, an analogy, or the prompting of a physical location or an act of embodiment—these bring us more easily and naturally to something suited to a living congregation rather than the reading eye.

Generally, I keep humor to the moment, because timing is simply better when you "feel" irony rather than "script" it. When composing a full manuscript allow space for impromptu speaking, particularly around personal stories, or small asides. These moments give the sermon its "fizz" and spontaneity in what is otherwise carefully composed. It also releases pressure for the listener, giving them a moment to breathe, regroup, and join along for the journey. Maybe just as important, it gives you a personal connection in that moment—the sermon isn't "tied to the manuscript" but rather like a kite, it has a string connecting it to an anchor even as it flits and lifts. The string is almost invisible—it is the kite, its swirls and dives, its surprise and delight, that captivates our reflection.

The string doesn't quite vanish. That's okay. That's true of all art, whether the art of the painter or the story of the novelist or the words of the poet or the prosthetic of the one who dances and sings.

Chapter Six

Coloring by Numbers

"There are no lines in nature, only areas of color, one against another."
—Edouard Manet

Going without maps is not all bad and may be a way we keep "rediscovering" the fun of a "new" path. But, by same the token, I've had experiences on the footpath where the map and compass were indispensable—heavy fog can make even familiar paths challenging. Or if your familiar path in the light of day becomes, by night, a noctambulant stranger, that too can become disorienting. Or perhaps when the land itself seems to lose its features.

That happened on the end of the Coast to Coast, as we approached Robin Hood's Bay: it was pastureland, flat and uninteresting. The footpath, which had been so sure and clear on the western side of the trail, where most people begin, had become faint to nonexistent, as fewer people complete the path on the far eastern end. Our progress was slow, with frequent stops to figure out "where" on the map we stood (most pastures look alike on a map). We found our way, only by the help of the map. But I was, as the British say, chuffed with myself for having led us to the precise T-junction indicated on Wainwright's map. That was a day when I was particularly glad that I knew how to use a map and compass.

Were it not for maps, I would seldom try any new paths for the simple reason of losing my navigational skills beyond a few familiar hikes. And if I really want to go somewhere over days or weeks or even months, my directional instincts won't carry me forward but might just leave me going in circles.

Cartography for the Sermon

What about preaching? Do we need a map and compass for the sermon? Perhaps we don't need a map for our "first" sermon. By that I mean, the sermon we preach almost by heart, because it represents our personal sermon. But much beyond that sermon, we begin to think, could I do better? Or, how might this practice become fresh to me? Or maybe we think, I've never really considered organizing a sermon, it just came naturally. But maybe you think, I might be able to do something different organizationally, but I've not got a lot to go on.

This chapter is about maps or reading them or how they can sometimes "read" or think back to us. In other words, when we look at an unfamiliar path on a map, we can see the path in an abstract way but it's while on the path that you begin to have a real dialogue between you, the pilgrim, and the map. The map "thinks" back—and in so doing it teaches us the art of the sermon and preaching life. A sermon form is a kind of map and, in a way, the homiletical equivalent to "coloring by numbers"—each number gets its prescribed color and, while at the beginning its logic seems obscure, by the end something materializes out of that number scheme. To treat preaching as if were coloring by numbers feels like cheating or perhaps trivializing. But without diminishing the mystery of preaching, a sermonic form, abstractly understood, invites us to discovery, as in all these little pieces add up into a distinctive picture that surprises us. We trust the innate logic of the scheme, but do not see or experience it until the final product. Similarly, understanding form in an abstract way and practicing it can help us learn the art of the preaching moment.

Part Two: Tinkering

Unity, Balance, Variety, and Movement

Broadly, we "map" a sermon using homiletical measurements of unity, balance, variety, and movement. Unity answers the question, Does the sermon "hold together" or is it "a string of pearls without any string"? As to balance or proportioning, we're looking for an even distribution between the description of our brokenness and richly textured content that speaks to God's healing and good news. Sermons often lack balance because ministers (like everyone else) find it easier to describe brokenness than healing. We keep good company: John Milton's *Paradise Lost* makes for better reading than his *Paradise Regained*. Mel Gibson's *Passion of the Christ* excels in violence and the Satan figure is vastly more interesting than the Christ figure—balance reminds us of what we're after. Variety emphasizes different modes and moods of communication, personal story, analogy, metaphor, logical exposition, aphorism, generationally specific sorts of references, and so on. The measure of movement goes to things that give the sermon its electricity, its jump. Does the message surprise us? Does it lead us to a reflective place? Does it challenge us to a different way of living or a better way of dying?

True North: Form and Function

Speaking of texts, is there an equivalent to the compass? It depends. Again, broadly speaking, a sermon's true north is orientated by the text as it bears witness to good news. It helps us to remember that while few of us find it easy to describe good news, that's our main thing. We speak of seriously imaginable vignettes or pictures of grace that are equal (in length and power) to the depictions of trouble or brokenness in the world. The Hegelian model of Samuel Proctor gives a one-third each of the sermon to antithesis (the brokenness of the world as we know it), thesis (the world as God intends it), and synthesis (our faithful response in reconciling the world's brokenness with God's healing and loving purpose)—by this standard, the Black tradition of preaching has more good news in it than most.[1] You don't want to leave a sermon crushed by "too much reality"—one experiences the uplift of the good news of God, a better word than that which we give to brokenness.

---

1. Proctor, *Certain Sound of the Trumpet*.

Coloring by Numbers

Good news, however, isn't a single thing, especially as we think about the text itself, the witness it makes. Each pericope comes to us in a literary form that points to the sermonic quality of good news. When we read the text in its literary form for the sermon, we may seek to "mimic" its mode (genre) but perhaps especially to mirror or recreate its function, what it effects.

Some Examples

What, we ask, does the pericope do? So, for instance, a passage from Proverbs comes in the form of aphorisms or memorable sayings. The writer of Proverbs seeks to reinforce a predictable universe: "Wise warriors are mightier than strong ones, and those who have knowledge than those who have strength" (24:5). It teaches that wisdom can be relied on, even in times of adversity or when it seems small compared to brute strength. Or it warns against bad behavior: "It is honorable to refrain from strife, but every fool is quick to quarrel. The lazy person does not plow in season; harvest comes, and there is nothing to be found" (20:3–4). Proverbial wisdom assumes a moral universe where good and responsible behavior is rewarded while bad behavior leads to an unhappy end. A sermon drawing on proverbial wisdom might find its true north in the idea that self-control and careful preparation yield rewards that we can rely on.

Switching to a destabilized universe, and guided by the reading strategies of Walter Brueggemann, we read Psalm 31.[2] Whereas the narrator of Proverbs enjoys a "stable moral universe" the writer of Psalm 31 speaks of a world splintered into pieces, sometimes trusting God (1–5): "In you, O Lord, I seek refuge; do not let me be put to shame. In your righteousness deliver me." And sometimes crushed with despair (9–13): "my life is spent with sorrow, and my years with sighing . . . I am the scorn of all my adversaries, a horror to my neighbors." The psalmist bookends the entire poem with assurance but does so while recognizing that simplistic formulas cannot be adequate by themselves. In this context, *reorientation* (rather than simplistic reiteration characteristic of a stable universe) may be the function of the psalmist—and the sermon.

When looking at the literary form of the parable, we see another function, namely the awakening of active thought. The parable of the dishonest manager in Luke 16:1–9 gives an example of this sort of thing. Although it may be difficult to reconcile ourselves to the idea that the dishonest

---

2. See Brueggemann, *Psalms and the Life of Faith*.

manager is a kind of Christ-figure, we recognize the implicit Christology at work:

- the dishonest manager lives under the rule of a capricious and unfair economic system: unsubstantiated charges were brought against this manager, but the "rich man" does not respond with equity and fairness but anger and retribution (1–2);
- the "dishonest" manager invents an "alternative" gift-economy, forgiving debts, welcoming hospitality (5–7);
- this alternative economy represents a winsome alternative and even the "master/rich man" comes to prefer it over the status quo (8).

What is the "true north" of a sermon emerging from this text? Clearly not to go commit financial fraud in Christ's name. Rather, to (1) expose the status quo as fraudulent, shortsighted, and contingent (it could be otherwise); (2) to "tease us into active thought" with winsome ways by which the practice of forgiveness of debts creates a meaningful economic alternative to financial systems that are normative for today.

Another way to make our way towards the form of the sermon is to reflect on what it effects. Texts spark, attack, or cause us to "turn aside" and seek understanding. They act on the listener in some way. But how? When reading, it might be helpful to think broadly of five "effects" of texts:

- Provoke: some stories or sayings put into question our sacred cows, they name the elephant in the room, they say, "This king has no clothes!" They challenge us to reckon with our collective acquiescence to injustice.

- Evoke: other pieces of Scripture, especially the Psalms or times when we hear a character, like Rebekah who says of her pregnancy with twins, "If this is the way it is to be, why do I live?" Or perhaps we hear Mark's story of Jesus' challenge to the rich person, but the "evocation" lingers with the verb: "Jesus looked at him and loved him"—it calls to mind or summons up a challenge that comes not from a place of impatience but rather a place of deep affection, care.

- Explain: The sayings of the psalmist and proverbial utterances offer clarifying (if somewhat overly neat) explanations of why things happen as they do. While avoiding simplistic explanations, the explanatory effects of texts support a congregation, giving clear guidance for those times in life when an aphorism or "saying" gets us through the next five minutes. For example, "an expectation is nothing more than a premeditated resentment" helps to "explain" the root of many resentful thoughts and attitudes and it is memorable and mostly true. The explanatory effect of Paul's writing shows itself in a more complex form. In the following excerpt, I compare power disruption brought on by a storm to Paul's explanation of how the Spirit intervenes, rendering the "power of the flesh" null and void:

> In a sense, you could read Paul's reflections in Romans 8 as a dramatic transfer of power to the Spirit of God in Christ, the power source for a new life illuminated by God's presence, giving us our life in the Spirit. Perhaps this is why Paul frequently repeats this "no longer" reality: we are "free from the law of sin and death" (2); we no longer "walk according to the flesh" (4); we do not set our minds on the flesh (6); "you are not in the flesh" (9); we are not "debtors to the flesh" (12); we do not "fall back into fear" (15). If the Spirit of Christ dwells in us, those switches and outlets that fueled our old identity have gone utterly dead—there is no power in them.

- Listen: In a sense, all texts ask us to listen, but some texts, particularly theophany texts, ask us to pause and to attend to the God who speaks in stillness—as an effect of Scripture, it is similar to the "evocation" function but with a more explicit feeling of alterity, of otherness of God and stranger asking us to hear their witness to an alternative world, or way of being. In this regard, consider examples that might incite an act of deeper listening: Elijah's experience of God speaking in the "sheer silence" (1 Kgs 19:12); Sarah hears a promise so outlandish that it generates something like cynical laughter (Gen 18:9–15); or perhaps the wordplay at work in the nocturnal visit of Nicodemus with Jesus comes to mind as prompting to listen twice (John 3:1–10).

- Remember and promise: Although these seem "separate" (one to do with the future and the other to do with the past) they call us to see our circumstances today in light of what God has done and what God promises to bring to completion. Some examples of the "remember and promise" effect of Scripture: Ezekiel's valley of dry bones (37:14); the "Servant Songs" of Isaiah (e.g., 42:1–4); the activity of remembering those who trusted God before us (Hebs 11).

Part Two: Tinkering

Your skills as a bricoleur should be in play here. Sometimes the bricolage surfaces the text before you've got the "function" and sometimes it happens after you've got the function. There's really no rule. What the image or metaphor does is give you a particular footpath to follow, giving you real contact with path and destination.

Sermon Forms

One step removed from the literary form and function of the text is a formal method of organizing the sermon. At the simplest level, sermonic forms, like the Hegelian form that I mentioned above, answer the question of how to "organize" the sermon. Sermon forms supply a map of the energies within a sermon: the energy of difficulty or trouble, the logical exposition of Scripture and the theological reflection that it generates, application and so on.

If your experience of sermonic forms is not quite sharp in your memory, that's not just you: many of us learned preaching from professors who viewed sermon forms in a negative light or as too light a subject for serious theological study. We don't color by numbers and perhaps we shouldn't preach that way either.

Or maybe we should preach by numbers, at least from time to time? Is there a slight discomfort with the language of forms in preaching? Poets use forms—haiku, iambic pentameter, prose—what are the sources of ambivalence about sermon forms? One point of discomfort comes from a reaction to a previous generation of homileticians that overprescribed one single sermonic form—a "glass slipper" to fit every sermon, every text, and every preacher. Closely related to this concern is the cornucopia of literary forms within Scripture—it seems peculiar to say that a "single" form is fit for purpose for every text.

Another negative influence on the study of the sermon form is the idea that all of us have within us the innate knowledge of how to organize a sermon. As teachers of preachers, it was our task to "midwife" the sermon that was within us to be born. This led to a way of teaching that may have touched on sermonic forms but so lightly that students never really learned a sermonic form as such. It is also based on a misunderstanding, that the sermon form that we have within us is a good form. It may be . . . and it may not be. You may hear sermons that sound remarkably like what someone learned from their preacher when growing up, or they draw from their previous life, perhaps as teachers or coaches. Teachers and coaches do, in fact, have a few "tools" in the bag and imitating a preacher from your experience is a time-honored way of learning to preach. Still, there's something off when we sound like our preacher back home. We would like something of our own voice in the preaching moment, but how do we get to that freedom? How do we find our own voice? Although it may feel counterintuitive, sermon forms play a role in finding our voice for the preaching moment.

The sermon form asks us to read the text through a particular structure, for a particular function. In this chapter we look at the map and compass of the sermon (1) through the broad dynamic of analogy and then (2) through the organizational schemes of different forms of the sermon, or what I'm calling "coloring-by-numbers" preaching.

Learning to Play

Analogy or perhaps "dynamic equivalence" between text and the world forms a basic pattern, a compulsion to map our world with the world of Scripture or to map Scripture with our world. At heart, it's a form of play, a bit like beginning on the footpath not quite knowing where it will lead you (it is an ancient text and you're a modern reader) but, in another way, the reader anticipates that the way recounted in Scripture (which cannot know you) knows you already. As for sermon forms, let's try coloring by numbers from time to time—sometimes we need something to kick-start our imagination. Alternatively, we can think of the sermonic form as a homiletical version of the haiku or acrostic or whatever poetic form you choose. A haiku takes our less-than-clear ideas and gives us a form to think through, to be born through. Sermon forms are like that. You have a text, an idea arising from that text, and then you find a sermon form and begin sieving that idea through the form. Very often, we'll be surprised by what the form helped to create.

When I said to my students that we should have "fun" in the preaching moment, many took exception, as if having "fun" were somehow not in keeping with the preaching moment. I disagree. To be clear, I don't believe preaching should be frivolous (and perhaps that's what they imagined when I said preaching should be fun) but I do believe it should be playful, which is to say psychologically limber rather than overly forced or too direct. Psychoanalyst D. W. Winnicott believed that serious play, a form of "fiction" in which we feel safe but in a real environment, was key to facing our inmost fears and hopes.³ And what is a sermon (with the pulpit as stage) but a form of theater (or therapy), where precisely the most important kinds of questions are approached? Yet, as Fred Craddock observes, if the preacher announces that all human beings are mortal, the congregation sleeps. When the preacher says that one of the saints of the church died in her sleep that night, it becomes the church. Craddock's insight goes to the way we respond to experience rather than exposition. We get closer to the deep thing (all humans are mortal) through some form of play. The only times when preaching can take leave of play is for the occasional sermon, where the occasion defines the sermon—for example a funeral or perhaps on Ash Wednesday or a local/national emergency. A crisis delivers its word of catastrophe and does so unmistakably. Yet, for the most part, there is a spirit of fun or mischief within the preaching moment, but it is fun with a serious purpose, namely getting at the profound questions that lay at the heart of the human condition.

Some Examples

People are natural children, but it takes a little bit of creativity, or a little bit of mischief (which is a species of creativity) to tickle that part of the human soul. One Sunday, my homiletical expression of "serious play" took the form of teasingly talking about leaving church. The text was Matthew's account of the astrologers' visit to see the infant Jesus (Matt 2:1–12). My beginning point for the sermon was nearer the end of the text, when the astrologers return home . . . which I "worked" for the fun of it. They didn't meet Jesus and change; they met Jesus and then went home. What I withheld in the "tease" part of the sermon above was Matthew's signal that the astrologers went home by *another* road, meaning under the influence of their encounter with the infant Jesus. Here's how it played out in the sermon itself:

> So the astrologers worshipped Jesus, gave him gifts of gold, frankincense, and myrrh. *And then went home.* The astrologers of Matthew, or the "magi" as they are more traditionally known, constitute the very first disciples of Jesus. And in that sense, they supply a model for us, as those who would follow Jesus. Which might pose a problem not because they go to see Jesus—which is good—but because they go home. And we never hear from them

3. Winnicott, *Playing and Reality*.

Coloring by Numbers

again. If the magi are any indication, Matthew wants us to leave church this morning. To go home and never come back.

So let's plan for this to be our last Sunday. Our going home Sunday. Not the Sunday when you die, but the Sunday when you take leave of this place. I know you've been thinking about it for a while. *I'm going leave this church. I'm going to do it.* That's usually a threat. But today, I think you should leave. Not right now, not while I'm preaching, please! But in about twenty minutes or so. And once you leave, I don't want you to come back. Don't send a forwarding address.

Is it so bad for me to say that? I mean, we are going to leave church today, aren't we? We will leave this church officially, maybe not today, maybe not tomorrow, but some day. We'll move. We'll transfer our membership. We'll drift away. We'll get angry and find somewhere better. We leave. And that shouldn't be so shocking. We do so, predictably, every Sunday. And today, we have biblical support for taking leave of this house where we meet Jesus, where we feel God's love, where we sing God's praise, where we meet and greet with God's family, it's good to be here.

And now it's time to leave, to go back to our country. It seems as if we're returning to the same country we left, by the same road we took, under the authority of the same ruler, our American Herod, perhaps. Our American Herod issues papers, doesn't he? Or he doesn't, depending. Papers are interesting things. Sometimes paper is what you carry in your pocket. Sometimes it's the color of your skin. Some colors get free passage. Some colors get profiled. Some orientations are stigmatized. It's pro forma, standard operational procedure, nothing personal, may I see your documents, please? *Or we're calling the police.*

When you travel under the authority of Herod, you take the road prescribed. Maybe something like the three astrologers from the east . . . but when they left Jesus, Matthew tells us they went by a different road, under another authority.

Eugene Lowry says that a sermon is like a narrative, it itches. Or, in the case above, it tickles and then it itches. Like a comedian, the beginning of the sermon violates a taboo that is supposedly sacrosanct: we seldom talk about leaving church in a playful way. Certainly, pastors loathe asking anyone to leave, ever, even when it would be best for everyone concerned. Please stay, we almost beg, while we pray quietly, please leave, please!

We take ourselves seriously, and the prospect or peril of our leaving we take even more seriously. Sometimes congregants threaten pastors with either leaving themselves or rumors that others have left. And preachers, too, play this card. The power of this threat is real but it's also comedic, especially if we juxtapose superficial acts of taking leave with the claim of the text. In this case, the claim of the text is that we leave church as disciples rather than the merely curious or frustrated. It also suggests, by way of function, that we leave our encounter with Jesus by a different path, a path other than Herod's.

Another sermon, this one on Ezekiel's valley of dry bones (Ezek 37:14), took a picture from our home life. Congregations generally know these texts as do most pastors; they often feel too familiar to generate curiosity on our part. The journey of the magi and the prophet's valley of dry bones are the equivalent of the familiar furniture in the house or the family pictures on the bookshelf. We wonder what, if anything, we can say about this sort of text. The point, however, is not to say something *about* the text, but to find the way the world gets into the text or the way the text sparks an insight into our world. Be assured: the very fact that familiar texts are familiar suggests that they possess within themselves an ability to awaken our eyes to the unfamiliar claim of the gospel. We only need to find the way of "striking" the text into existential fire. And playfulness is one of the most effective forms of locating that existential fire. So, in this message on Ezekiel's dry bones, I engaged in another analogy, comparing my sermons to the dry bones confronting the prophet:

> About a week ago I decided it was cold enough to justify building a fire—I went looking for an old newspaper, but there wasn't any to be found. As I was pondering my situation, I noticed an old sermon, paper-clipped together and still inside its bulletin, sitting on the shelf in what we call the reading room. I think it was a sermon called "Stirrings in the Night"—but it wasn't stirring anymore. It had passed from stirring to rigor mortis and even beyond. All its moisture was gone; all the oil of Holy Spirit sanctification vanished; all the sweat of prayer, all the little notes and reminders written in the margin, meant nothing to me now. It's days of stirring—either on Sunday or any other day were over! I took it, and page by page, twisted it into thin tubes of paper, thirteen or fourteen pages all told, enough for a fire.
>
> Imogen and Gwendoline walked in and saw what I was doing: "Are you burning your sermon?" they demanded.
> "Yes," I said, "I am!"
> "Really?" they asked, astonishment rising in their voices. "Your sermon? You're burning your sermon?!" Then they sprinted

down the stairs, crying out, "Daddy's burning his sermon!" And it was true, that's exactly what I was doing. I was beginning to see the poetic potential of my act . . . "Yes," I said, "my sermon is really on fire now!" Which sent the girls into a fit of giggles—they ran downstairs and yelled out to mom, "Daddy's sermon is on fire! Daddy's sermon is on fire!"

They found this immensely amusing—as in, perhaps they don't always think so, as in fire and daddy's preaching isn't a natural association—but there it was, a sermon on fire, with licks of bright lively flame, sizzling up the stove pipe, promising warmth to one and all.

Reading Ezekiel's vision of the valley of dry bones put me into a metaphorical mood—and I wondered about those pages, those dry sermonic salvages, and I thought, "What of the sermon that we write each day of our lives? How is that sermon going? Is there any life in it? Or our lives, are they just the accumulation of days, of dry days, days insensible to season, deaf to feeling, twenty-four hours repeating, a monotonous valley, without narrative or name or purpose?

The first two examples have an analogical connection to the text:

- leaving church | astrologers go home (they leave Jesus);
- dry pages of human life | a valley of dry bones.

An analogy does not rope the text with a one-to-one correspondence to the preacher's particular agenda—it represents an allusive or associative connection, not a prescriptive one. Allegories, a close cousin to the analogy, reduce the text to a symbol for something else: Origen, the master of allegory, allegorizes Jacob's ladder into rungs of spiritual progress. Each rung, in the allegory, represents one step in our spiritual formation. The ladder of Jacob, whatever that meant, is completely colonized by the allegory—and it was still a good sermon.

I prefer the analogy's loose connection to the text. An analogy offers a loose connection to the meaning of the text. It stands alongside it and says this feels somehow similar—not identical but kindred in spirit. By contrast, the allegory overprescribes meaning to the text, as if the text were an empty container waiting passively to be filled by the imagination of the preacher. The text as text makes analogy interesting without being overbearing (it isn't "exactly" like the text) while allegorical approaches harness a good idea (spiritual formation) to an unsuspecting text. Allegorical sermons inadvertently short-circuit the way a close reading of the text probes our experience. There is a residue of allegory in the analogical take on the text—the burning sermon manuscript comes very close to allegorizing—and that's okay. We still want to interpret the text as text, for how the author intended it for their readers. However, reading Scripture in an analogical way honors the way generations have experienced the meaning of Scripture, as in some way giving symbolic shape to our human experience.

An analogy like the two above requires an "extra step" of the imagination, a creative connection that doesn't always appear obvious to the listener, and that's not because the listener is dense but because the listener is alert. In both instances, the analogical connection requires an imaginative leap, especially on the part of the listener who is in a position of guessing how text and image/narrative are analogues to one another. It should be a strong and clear connection. Those may be two reasons to exercise care with the analogical mode of preaching: (1) it requires an extra leap of the imagination; (2) it may not be self-evidently arising from the text. Of course, the reason the analogical leap works is because the text intends allusive and evocative readings rather than explanatory or prescriptive ones. The text itself includes a "wink" and "peek" sort of logic, with or without our analogies.

Sermon forms are not simply abstract structures by which to organize a sermon. They include a theological understanding of how human beings talk about themselves. They do so through story or through intrinsic dynamics of the gospel story (transformation, liberation), or through a logical reading of the text (exposition, theological reflection, application).

Another way of thinking about a sermonic form is as a series of theological questions or parameters through which, in an abstract way, interpreters think through the evolution of the claim of a text. In the following sermon beginning, I dig into the problem of Jesus' age in the visit to the temple in Luke 2:41–52. Analogy exists just beneath the surface, but the text and its narrative dynamic is inescapably the catalytic spark. Jesus' age is the "wink" and "peek" of the sermonic idea (maybe the analogy) which is developed as an "itch" or "curiosity" within my interpretation of the text. This models Eugene Lowry's narrative loop: itch, ouch, aha (gospel clue), yeah, and celebration (he uses more sophisticated terms but these, also Lowry's, are more memorable).[4]

---

4. Lowry, *Homiletical Plot*.

Coloring by Numbers

Itch | Luke tells us that it was the time of year when everyone traveled to Jerusalem for the Passover. They did this every year, like clockwork. In fact, Luke repeats this formula, saying they went up "as usual"—just like always. They knew where they'd be going, with whom they would travel, what they would eat, what they would do the day after the celebration. They always did the same thing, with the same people, at the same time every year [*extending the vowels, imitating the inflections of a "teenager voice" giving voice to exquisite boredom with family traditions*]. But our writer introduces the first whiff of a problem in this story of every year, same thing, same time, same place, same boring people. The problem: Jesus is twelve years old. Some of you, if you're closer to twelve years of age, get why hanging out with parents might be boring—you maybe are also wondering why being twelve years old would be a problem. That's a good question. We'll get to that so-called "problem" in a moment, but why does Luke specifically portray Jesus as twelve years old? One possibility is that it would have been the year before Jesus would have been "graduated" into the adult world of Judaism, which was age thirteen for boys. Today, we may know about the bar mitzvah or the bat mitzvah (for girls). This precise ritual didn't exist at Jesus' time, but the idea was there. And some believe that Joseph and Mary, as people of faith, would have taken Jesus to the temple rituals earlier, to expose him to the traditions before he was of age.

Ouch | Whatever the reason, Luke tells us that they did this as usual. And Jesus is just about a teen. *As in, maybe Mom and Dad are going to get a little surprise. To be a teen is the definition of unusual, or at least unpredictable. And Jesus does not disappoint in the unpredictable category.* What does he do? Jesus stays behind in Jerusalem. And his parents didn't know it. What they thought they knew was in fact what they imagined to be true. They continued the trip home with the idea that Jesus was with them, with the extended family and friends of their community; they imagined Jesus with them as though it were an established fact. But at some point, somewhere along the line, someone asked the question: "Where's Jesus?"

"I don't know. I thought he left with you."

"No, he didn't leave with us. We thought he was with you."

Then the rush to look for Jesus, at first among their relatives and friends. And they didn't find him. Finally, they do find Jesus. *Where*? In the temple. Doing what and with whom? Listening to highly regarded teachers, asking questions, almost a model of polite adolescence. Relief, right? . . . a good boy? Or maybe not

Part Two: Tinkering

quite good, or at least the way we conceive good. In a sense, Joseph and Mary don't find the Jesus they knew but the Jesus they had not yet comprehended. Even Mary, the one who receives the theological sonogram that told her everything about Jesus, Mary didn't get *who* Jesus was. When his parents finally find him, Mary says a little insultingly, "Child"—it's a bit like how a mom might say, Robert Paul, I brought you into this world, I can take you out of it—"Child," she says, "why did you do this to us? We were worried sick about you!"

Aha | Jesus' answer to his parents is twofold. The first is a question, the first words he speaks in the Gospel of Luke: "Why were you searching for me?" And the second was, "Did you not know that I must be in my Father's house?"

If you've been exposed to narrative models of preaching, you will recognize this approach to the text: the narrative approach lifts what seems at first like a curiosity or an itch and pursues that itch until there's some kind of clue to the resolution, which signals the turn in the sermon towards the good news. As form, it invites us to linger with the itch, develop it, don't relieve it by saying, "This text teaches us the lesson of Jesus being so much larger than anything we can contain or hold"—this is true, but it is also boring. Scratch until you begin to draw blood.

This sermon example cuts from where the text introduces the "clue" to the resolution, namely, Jesus' two questions. I've since forgotten what I did with this sermon, but if I were to revisit it again (I might), I think I'd move to the "celebration" by naming other ways in which the adolescent Spirit of Jesus captivates (insubordinates) and surprises us in Luke's Gospel. Maybe we could start with resurrection (a typically teenage stunt), or maybe we touch on the quick intelligence Jesus applies to stale arguments and cynical questions, or perhaps Jesus' ability to be vulnerable in ways that adults find difficult. A story about the surprising intelligence, gifts, and beauty of a so-called "problem" age might appropriately follow.

The beauty of this approach is that the sermon form leads to an enlivened exposition of the text as opposed to an authoritative exposition of the text or a proposition about some accepted truth developed in several points. The narrative path, the one we mutually care about, helps both preacher and congregation discover the good news. Yet some will say that the narrative model isn't quite showing all its cards: the preacher already knows the "clue" and yet, by art of story, conveys the spontaneousness of discovery. The mistake in this criticism is assuming that we learn our human experience in any other way—story, to paraphrase Pierre Teilhard de Chardin, gets us involved in what it means that we are spiritual beings undergoing a human experience. It is no accident that most of Scripture and the whole sweep of it together meets us as a story. Biblical narratives excite living truth, which is frankly elusive and allusive, rather than expositing flat dogmas, which are stored in stacks.

So that's my vote for narrative approaches to preaching.

How does it compare with the analogical beginnings above? In my analogical approaches, the human need is paramount, feelings of a life wasted, a purpose scattered, a desire to leave, to slam the door and never come back. So, we think about leaving church, that's one thing. But how do we leave as disciples? That's another thing. No, the text isn't explicitly (or even vaguely) about how people leave church, though it is about how the encounter with Christ changes those who continue the path of discipleship.

The dry pages idea for Ezekiel was more explicitly therapeutic: sometimes we feel as if the sermon of our life, the day-in-day-out drudgery of work and relationships, is less than vivified and vivifying. Ezekiel's vision is a historic crisis; my analogy was unapologetically personal. In my defense, Ezekiel's valley of dry bones belongs to the "ravishing" genre of biblical narratives—it richly blesses not only those who get its historical context but those who simply touch the delicate hem of the renewal that it promises. Both analogies honor the way people come to church: they may be thinking about the future, how they will leave the church (perhaps existentially); they may not be thinking when they come, "My life isn't feeling very lively" but the Ezekiel text, as a good therapist, stirs that up for us. It's the preacher's responsibility to raise that feeling to the surface.

While many people jettison writing their sermons, it allows you to revisit something, to see where you're struggling or to make a connection. I frequently find the "beginning" of the sermon midway through a draft composition, sometimes made on Tuesday or Wednesday. Often you don't "find" the itch except in drafting—and that goes for the "wink" or the clue to the gospel.

Incidentally, I don't speak of the "authority" of Scripture. Why? Because I am also happy to "map" my experience onto Scripture. It's a perfectly human thing to do. But, at the end of the day, the text gives shape to my shapelessness. Without it, I am turning without a center. With it, I find a place to call holy ground, to start again.

Part Two: Tinkering

Neither underestimate the congregation's interest in the theological content of Scripture nor misinterpret that interest. We're looking for a theological and christological framework. The sermon vivifies the mind with a theological angle rather than merely educating it. A vivid, lively encounter with the drama of God in Scripture is both more instructive and more faithful to the actual text, which, after all, often comes in the form of narrative. Having said that, the truth is there is an analogical component in the narrative arc of the Luke example, but it is less pronounced than the examples from Ezekiel and Matthew.

Now here's something to consider: none of these "beginnings" came to me on Monday, or Tuesday, Wednesday. At best, they came to me on Thursday, or perhaps, more often, on Friday morning. I wish more books on homiletics would simply say that: our final product, the video of the "great sermon" or "Exhibit A" always seems like the obvious fruit of our labor, and it was low hanging fruit. Preaching, we may conclude, is easy. Just pull down that peach of a sermon and soon your homiletical mouth will be dripping with the sweet nectar of sanctification. Or not. The best kept secret of the preacher is that the finest of what we hear on Sunday is the cream of our weekly labors. What I gave above are two examples of glimpsing the Lion Inn. That's what it looks like! It's warm. It's inviting. It's just a little way up over that hill . . . just out of sight.

The Black tradition of preaching gives us the dialectal approach of Samuel Proctor, an approach I learned through James Harris, a remarkable preacher and proponent of the dialectical theology of the Black tradition.[5] Harris, one of Proctor's students, believes that the scriptural story holds within it a dialectal dynamic, a way of exploding or liberating oppressive systems and that the Hegelian model helps us to exploit the explosive power of Jesus' story as liberation for the captive. He also told me, over a cup of coffee, that if I was ever short on time, in a busy week in the ministry, the thesis-antithesis model provides a quick and easy-to-read map—or a way to preach by numbers.

So what does the dialectal approach look like in practice? I've sketched out an example, loosely based on Jesus' inauguration sermon in Luke 4:16–30: It consists of three major parts and one question that arises from the first two moves. This is not the sermon, but its dialectical flow:

> Thesis | We're looking for the way God creates the world; the way resurrection reality renews the creation. This is not the moment of

---

5. See Harris, *Preaching Liberation*.

"ought" but "is"—the world as God creates it. Jesus bears witness to this "is" when he completes the reading from Isaiah, sits down (the traditional teaching position) and announces the reality inbreaking at that moment: "Today this scripture has been fulfilled in your hearing" (21). Jesus' "is" invites the congregation to think about the way the world is if the gospel (or claim of the text) *is* true: in that world, the dead do rise, the sick revive with wholeness, the captives rejoice in freedom, the poor have good news preached to them and are no longer poor, so good is the news. If the Scripture is true.

That "if" casts an implicit shadow over the sermon. It begs the question. It may be easier to start with the antithesis since that names the feeling of the hurt or injury in the world. That's mostly where preachers start, but if worship is a form of celebration, as it is in the Black tradition, you might begin best in a spirit of rejoicing before moving to explore, in the strength of that dialectical movement, to that which opposes Christ's announcement that the word of freedom is fulfilled in our hearing. If you struggle with the thesis language, think of the confessional language of the church—it will be tempting to say what the world "ought" to be like. But the dialectal power of thesis propels us into that synagogue where freedom speaks easily and with compelling power for those who believe.

Antithesis | In the antithesis, we describe the world as it is when we pretend as if the gospel (or claim of the text) is not true: justice is deferred, the dead stay dead, the captives are never released, people who are sick can't get healthcare, and people live under a paralyzing burden of unrelenting poverty. Describing the problem or brokenness of the world comes more easily than the thesis language so you will want to keep it roughly in balance with the thesis movement. But up to this point, you have only given a diagnosis of the disease—the rupture that has come because human beings do terrible things to one another, denying the possibility of resurrection in our world. As you move to the Relevant Question (below) and the synthesis, you begin to treat the sickness, not just its symptoms but the root issue or problem, with a gospel remedy.

Relevant Question | The relevant question begins the treatment and it begins with a form of repair, seeking to reconcile the world of resurrection and freedom with the world of death and captivity. Out of that reconciliation, we get glimpses and foreshadows of the new creation. So, perhaps, we ask, how does the God (claim of the text) of Scripture ask us to reconcile these two binaries so that we have a coherent vision of God's alternative rule breaking out in our world? Incidentally, one thing that this form taught me was how the relevant question works, underlining the difference between a barrage of questions (demonstrating rhetorical dominance) and one or two thoughtful questions for the formation of our souls (a better kind of rhetoric).

Synthesis | Apply the thesis as an instrument of liberation medicine for the sickness of a world where justice is deferred, etc. Often, this is where a story from contemporary life is helpful. Such a story tells a narrative that is gritty and realistic, but also hopeful, being lifted by a hope that comes from something as mystical as resurrection in this life.

Does antithesis/thesis sound like a strange language for a sermon idea? It did when I was first introduced to it. Yet that strangeness aided in the development of a sermon with dynamic theological content: I had to stop and ask, what does antithesis mean relative to the claim of this text? What alternative reality does the writer testify to as a basic expression of the real and vital force of the resurrection narrative? What question helps us begin to reconcile these two opposites?

Obviously, your creativity comes into play—you read a text and you as a person "color in" the form or structure. My use of this model is not identical to James Harris's, but it does show a family resemblance. You will need to try it more than once if you want to be confident using it. However, once you master it, if you ever need a color by numbers sermon on Sunday, you simply fill in the blanks.

Eugene Lowry once said to us that we were never called to "preach the lectionary" but to preach the gospel. It was one of those moments from preaching class that stays with you for a lifetime. Thinking about it now, the same goes for sermonic forms, including Lowry's itch, ouch, aha, riding the wave, and yeah!—we're not called to preach forms but that Christ means freedom. Forms are easy, like coloring by numbers. Freedom is difficult, perhaps impossible apart from the grace of God.

But I still enjoy coloring by numbers.

Signposts for the Footpath

Shane McCrae, a poet, observes this about his emerging identity as a Christian—and it coincides with his birth as a formalist poet:

> I came to a sense of myself as a Christian around the time I came to a sense of myself as a formalist poet. My relationship with theology and my relationship with poetry are, in some ways, both searching for ways to think, spaces in which to think. When I started writing sonnets, it became easier to think in poetry; whereas when I was surrounded by what people think of as freedom and could make whatever decisions I wanted—my lines could be as long or short as I wanted and bear no necessary relationship to each other—it was very difficult to do any kind of thinking. *I was constantly worrying about the wrong things.*

McCrae then connects the "abstract" quality of form with the dialogical experience of living and thinking through that form:

> Theology is another space in which it is possible to think, because there is a framework against which my thoughts are bouncing and by which they're being shaped. Thinking about Jesus, thinking about God, is in some ways a lot like thinking about a sestina, because you have parameters. I know, generally speaking, how a sestina works; I can kind of talk about it. But how I think through my relationship with those parameters is new every time I encounter them. It's shaped by the sestina being what a sestina is in some abstract way. And so I can approach it and think about it, *and it thinks back.* That's how it works for me.[6]

Reading his account recalled for me a student who had struggled through the preaching class. At the time, we were practicing developing grace notes in the sermon. As I listened to one of their final sermons, I felt as if I was witnessing something like a breakthrough. Something that happened in the sermon and, indeed, after it, when we were all seated in a circle for critique. He had not been a shining star in the class but when he came to the grace functions—the parameters of this sermonic form—his voice and

---

6. Smith, "Obliqueness," 57 (my italics).

expression grew warm and full of kindness. I asked him about it afterwards, observing back to him what I saw in him, not only what he said but how he had said it, and how different it had seemed from previous attempts. It was, I said, a grace-filled moment.

"You were smiling as you spoke. I hadn't seen that before. Where," I asked, "did that warmth come from?"

"It's what I believe," he said, still smiling. Did the form, abstractly understood, think back in its final sermonic expression? Did thinking through the parameters of a "color-by-numbers" scheme release one person from worrying about the wrong things while also liberating him to bear witness to the truest thing we should ever know?

PART THREE

Community

Chapter Seven

Wee Gaggles

"The reading of a fine book is an uninterrupted dialogue in which the book speaks and our soul replies."

—Andre Maurois

I AM NOW PAST the midpoint of life, and I'm not as fleet of foot as I was when I was younger. Getting to the top of a peak like the Scottish Highlands' Cairngorm, 1,245-meters, takes more than physical strength; it takes a generous capacity to stop, take in the views, and breathe. Or in short, to rest. But it's more than rest, isn't it? If you're an admirer of the English walker Wainwright's guidebooks, you'll recall his sketches of mountains and valleys of the Lake District, all exceptionally detailed. They say you can almost depend just on his guide and sketches as navigation tools, given the care that he took to describe the path. As I think about it, "How did he do it? How did he sketch these careful pictures of peaks and valleys?" Simple, really: he had to stop. But these were more than interruptions or an opportunity to refuel. Wainwright's sketches and style of narrating tell me that being absorbed by the place, where we have come, even when we have not yet arrived, is important to our whole experience.

Part Three: Community

This pencil drawing by my oldest daughter, Gwendoline, is of the Three Peaks of Yorkshire, a footpath that includes Ingleborough, Whernside, and Pen-y-ghent. Rebecca and I completed it in a little over twelve hours—failing to meet the threshold of twelve hours or less to become official three-peakers. Maybe that is why, when I see this sketch, I think of losing the path near Whernside, the steep climb up Ingleborough, the mist making it impossible to reach its trig-point (the highest point on the peak), the Roman road at the end, and the loss of one of my toenails, only discovered after I took off my socks when we got back home.

A much more pleasant memory was the Brontë Walk, named after the Brontë sisters. As a family, we hiked about eight of its forty miles. When the Brontë Walk comes up in conversation, we often remember its *stops* or the wee gaggles that punctuate our memories: the way we explored some of the buildings, in ruins now, that the Brontës called home; the way we marveled at the shark's tooth that our second oldest daughter found (and soon lost); the patch of green grass where we had lunch and then took a short afternoon nap; the litter of Border collies with whom we visited; and now that I'm writing, how one of the women on the farms took us on a detour from the official path so that we would avoid a field with a bull. In other words, what we often take from the footpath is not so much a destination but a discovery or discoveries along the way. Isn't this also true of preaching, that we see or feel things, we discover or lose something, we take something with us, a prized possession of the soul?

Another experience is that of the paradigm shift or a shift that is both simultaneously subtle and monumental. I experienced the latter while on the Cumbria Way, which runs from south to north through the middle of the Lake District all the way to Carlisle, just south of Scotland. For the first part of the Cumbria Way, the rivers flow in a southerly direction, against your progress. You get used to seeing this pattern of things and then, when you cross over the Langdale Pikes, the streams begin to flow with you rather than against you. There's no flashing light to announce that you've crossed a watershed point between north and south. You're on a peak. You look out to where you've been, in the south and, with a simple turn, you're looking north to where you're going. The irony is that you can see everything except perhaps the most significant thing, which is directly under your feet, a fundamental shift in the topography. Only as you continue down the footpath do you notice the streams and then the river that flows in the opposite direction to which you've grown accustomed. I'm guessing there are some walkers who never notice it at all—it represents a massive change, on a scale that we don't always recognize in the very moment. In ministry, do we sometimes pass through a basic change, so fundamental that it shapes our experience but also so vast that perhaps we don't "see" it unless prompted to do so? I will explore these as "inflection" points in the journey of a community of faith.

What follows in this chapter: (1) examples of "wee gaggles" and (2) where and how we might find and identify "inflection points" in our interpretive life within congregations.

Wee Gaggles

The idea of a wee gaggle was suggested to me by a friend from seminary, Linda Pollock. I shared with her that I felt exhausted—those were very close to my words—at the end of Sunday services, not because of the physical/psychic energy of the exertion of leading worship but primarily because the service (its richness) had become so transactional. In other words, for some in the congregation the sermon was a way station where they "refueled" for the week and for others a necessary road-crossing on the way to brunch—the latter group endured the sermon. The refueling group valued the sermon in the same way they might value a stop at the petrol station—you don't visit with the proprietor or particularly show interest in larger questions of clean energy or climate change. A smaller group wanted to engage around the sermon but had neither the context nor the framework for that kind of conversation. And there was, of course, me, standing in the narthex, doing the minister thing on Sunday, wondering what, if anything, was percolating in the life and imagination of the church—I was part of this "smaller group." Linda suggested I try a wee gaggle after the service. "Keep it informal," she said. "Just a short conversation over tea and biscuits." What I suggest below develops Linda's idea further.

So, what is a "wee gaggle"? Let's begin by saying what it isn't: the wee gaggle is not the critique of the sermon or even you as the preacher—you may listen that way, or "overhear" critique, but that's not its point. A wee gaggle and a sermon critique in homiletics are two different things—homiletics, or the art of sermon-making, is related but distinct from the wee gaggle. The wee gaggle belongs to the congregation or to congregational formation. The wee gaggle seeks depth as it operates in the semi-structured space of questions and reflections prompted by a sermonic event. Positively, maybe the wee gaggle is a kind of space that allows a collective "aha" moment, where the participants surface the drama of the gospel in a more down-to-earth key.

We're interested in the *what* of the listener's response, or to questions that rise to the level of formation and discipleship, or who we are because of who Christ is. These go beyond talking "about" a sermon—the listener's response goes to questions about our experience of God, ourselves, and neighbor. Basically, we're trying to capture here, in a way appropriate for our time, the way of testimony. Books, while we love them, do not explicitly ask for our participation in their narratives. The Christian narrative, however, has its, "Go and do likewise." Our narratives ask us to publicly, practically, and personally to engage with the Word proclaimed. We don't often go there, not because sermons do not merit active engagement at that level or that there aren't responses and questions like these, but because, in part, we haven't created space for that kind of conversation. Or the example that we do have, the "testimony," does not feel right for so many different reasons. And yet, ignoring that impulse, we almost treat congregational response to the sermon as a potentially radioactive substance and we lock it into the lead-lined box of the car ride home.

By contrast, if you read the letters of American novelist Flannery O'Connor, you eavesdrop on her spirited conversations with her readers, reviewers, and friends. Preachers live with their congregations and a sermon becomes an expression of that life together, not unlike O'Connor's relationship to her readers. Sometimes we do not quite know how to engage with a sermon beyond the transaction—good sermon, bad sermon, where-are-we-meeting-for-lunch sermon. And some of that is down to consumerism in the church and some to fear or anxiety of the preacher or the listener who doesn't want to offend or doesn't have the framework to speak or think in that moment. If I'm the preacher, I might ask, what will they say? Or, if I'm a layperson, I might question whether there's anything for me to say at all, or is this safe?

Some Suggestions

I have struggled with the formational problem of preaching for most of my teaching and preaching life and I still do. We "feel" a sermon (or not), assess a sermon (good or bad), we protect the soft tissue (our own) once the sermon is loosed, we get a biscuit and a cup of tea and talk about the weather or anything but the sermon. And yet the sermon lingers at the center of most of our services, this awkward teenager, who can't be missed but would like to hide. Wee gaggles help. Just as on the footpath, where conversations are born without premeditation, we will sometimes find that a wee gaggle opens us to conversation in the space of a sermonic journey. Wee gaggles are ways for us to honor what is already there and, at the same time, return the sermon to its native home, the testimony of people of faith. Gaggles are in time, week in or week out. They focus on the transience of a text, a sermon, some pilgrims sharing a road together. The questions below are designed to spark ideas for how you might incorporate meaningful congregational engagement with the sermon. The questions enable a small group to practice the art of hearing the sermon together—we hear more than we can say but what we can say is still important for our collective formation. Thoughtful questions help create a safer space so we can gain depth as listeners.

    Wee gaggles can take place either within the sermon itself or following the sermon, either through social media, or using a survey-type tool, or during fellowship. My suggestions below could be situated . . .

Part Three: Community

- as "Responding to the Word Proclaimed" (a form of discipleship where the congregation may eavesdrop on three people answering the questions);
- in the sermon itself (a modification of the dialogue sermon);
- or following the sermon, during a fellowship time;
- or with the use of an online "survey" adapted for spiritual formation rather than customer satisfaction.

These conversations take place in the ebb and flow but, given the scattering of our lives, perhaps a gently curated dialogue will help each of us grow.

Some might ask, "Why not simply reconceive the sermon in the form or genre of a 'talk' with back-and-forth between preacher and listener?" The wee gaggle is my slight variation on that theme. In this variation, I aim for three things: first, to conserve the sermonic footpath, something those who live with sermons continue with as a guide and facilitator of interpretation. The footpath of the preacher has something to teach us. A monologue can be a bore, of course. But spend a little time with preachers like Barbara Lundblad or Fred Craddock—and you'll be glad they gave themselves to the path, listening to its message. But here's the thing: even as you listen, a good sermon engenders conversation, dialogue about things that matter most. With the wee gaggle, you get depth as well as breadth.

My second concern goes to a shared thirst for collective recognition and personal formation in a more intimate context—there is a tension here, between the sermon carefully and dialogically crafted, and the idea of the sermon as literal conversation. Putting my cards on the table, I'm not persuaded that "conversational" preaching—where the preacher poses questions for group conversation or asks questions while preaching—is as conversational as it purports to be nor as reflective as a traditional sermon can be. But I do want experimentation at the intersection of the monologue-chatty binary. The conception of the wee gaggle is my contribution to this question.

In designing wee gaggle questions, avoid assessment—assessment belongs in another context. Seek a positive pastoral shape for the question. Design questions that open us to reflection and just living. Formulate questions that help the people of God see and report good news as it appears in ordinary life.

General questions might be adapted or used. Without using the word "doctrine," you might want to identify the human concern that doctrine

Wee Gaggles

tries to answer, recalling that doctrine, at its best, is a kind of medicine cabinet for pastoral theologians and their congregations. The doctrine of creation, for example, treats the dis-ease of what it means that we exist, or for the purpose of and our relationship to other created things; covenantal doctrine speaks to God's promise to the world and our promise to God and one another; the doctrine of mission includes theologies of evangelism and social witness, among others. You may identify the doctrine of sovereignty as relevant to the church community undergoing transition or that a doctrine of creation helps a congregation undertake its greening initiatives.

As for the questions themselves, the main thing is that they are open-ended and treat the sermon/text as a catalyst, as a spark for formation. They activate thought in a personal way. Do you distinguish between the sermon and the Scripture reading? You might do so ... or you might use the "Scripture reading" as synonymous with the sermon. Some listeners will engage with the text directly, either because they have the training, or they have that disposition. But most will hear the sermon *as* the Scripture reading. The sermon begins to answer the congregational question, "How do you read it?" But in a wee gaggle, the people respond to that question in their way. In terms of process, if done following the sermon during fellowship, you might read all the questions and ask the group to choose one or two they want to think about in twenty or so minutes. These are generic but maybe helpful in your own composing:

- What challenged or surprised you in today's Scripture reading?
- What gave you hope or courage?
- Does the story or stories from the Bible readings today describe people like you? Why or why not?
- Think about this question: How will my life be different now?

For a sermon on forgiveness, try these questions for a start:

- What makes an apology substantial rather than superficial?
- How is forgiveness a gift? How is it a burden?
- Is it easier to give forgiveness or to receive it? Why?

General questions come from a pastoral reading of doctrine. Doctrine is not, after all, for the professional theologian but for our human formation.

A particular sermon offers its own questions. An indirect benefit of formulating questions goes to sermon development. Ask yourself, "If this

Part Three: Community

sermon were two or three open questions, what would they be?" If you find it difficult to identify those questions, you might want to check with your homiletical editor to clarify focus and function. Do you have a clear claim of the text on human life and the world? In other words, if the witness of Scripture were true, what would the world look like as a result? Relatedly, what do you, as pastor and interpreter of Scripture, hope to achieve or change because of this sermon? A clear answer to these two questions is essential for the wee gaggle.

A wee gaggle shifts gears from homiletics to human formation, or an exercise in personal and congregational formation in small group reflection. Is this one step too many in an already tight schedule? Perhaps enlist a trusted person in your circle who can hear your sermon and distill it down to a question or two for a wee gaggle—that might relieve you of some of the legwork and there might be a surprise or two as you listen in the life of the sermon beyond its twenty minutes of glory.

For a sermon on Jeremiah 18:1–11, the parable of the potter's house, I settled on this theme: "The Spirit uses God's divine hands to reshape mishapen lives into lives that give happiness to us and joy to the world God so loves". An excerpt from the sermon:

> One lesson of the parable of the potter's house is that we may not be able to avoid making mistakes—remember that you heard it here first! We will make mistakes. That's basic. But the deeper lesson may be that we misunderstand the nature of those mistakes. The French philosopher Gabriel Marcel distinguishes between a problem and a mystery. A problem, he tells us, is something we view from the outside. The windowpane is broken. This is what it needs to be repaired. That's a problem. But a mystery is something in us, not outside. It can't be fixed; it can only be lived. Maybe getting tied up in knots, going through setbacks, heartache, and heartbreak—maybe that's part of this whole being human thing. Our life, the good and the bad, isn't a problem to be fixed but a mystery to be lived. Here's a question for you: Do you know how many times you've fallen today? That's a trick question, because I hope you said, "I didn't fall"—but, on the other hand, even if you didn't fall, maybe in another sense you did. Laurie Anderson, in her poem "Walking and Falling" says that each time we take a step, we fall.[1] And each time you fall, you catch yourself, you fall, you catch yourself, you fall—we call it walking. Someone else might call it falling if they didn't know any better. If I could listen to the

1. Anderson, "Big Science."

lesson of my own body, that it teaches me that falling is very close to walking, how might I face other "fails" in my life?

For this sermon on change, failure, and our formation as unique human beings, these were the questions I used in the wee gaggle:

- What feelings do I experience when I think I have failed?
- When have I grown in an experience of failure?
- When others fail, I am learning that . . .

If you were to incorporate the wee gaggle into a five-minute "response to the Word proclaimed" or a two- or three-minute "introduction" to the sermon, give some thought to whose experience will raise congregational conscience and congregational consciousness. Would it be helpful to hear from one kind of group or a diverse group? What benefits might there be in posing these questions to one person? What might be the risks?

Christ the King Sunday (Year C) assigns Luke's account of Jesus' crucifixion at Luke 23:33–43. Verse 33b lingered with me: "they crucified Jesus there with the criminals." In the sermon for that day, I returned to this image:

> Do you know that when Luke says that Jesus was crucified *and the criminals with him*—that means with us? That leads me to ask, what crucifies us? What separates us? Bitter rivalries? Shame? Injuries we have inflicted? Injuries inflicted on us? What separates us? Maybe it's every day that I can't say I love you, even though with all my being that is the only thing I want to say. Every day I can't say, I'm sorry. Every day that I can't be with you, even though with all my being I long to be with you. Crosses that we die on . . . everywhere, in every life. No one is excluded. Not even Jesus, "there with the criminals." The difference? In that "Jesus there with the criminals," the power of the cross to define is destroyed. Jesus speaks of a "today" not as the victim of the cross but as one who reigns from an upside-down throne. He says that what we long for every day is, by God's grace, ours today. Today, I love you. I today, I tell you I'm sorry, today, I am with you, today, even though we die, we live.

Luke's account of Jesus' crucifixion narrates the way Jesus' life joins our life at every point. The cross signifies the far end of the everyday nature of Jesus' ministry—Jesus lives alongside us, fully exposed to shame, alienation, living with the inability to take back injury and perhaps even the inability to recognize the pain our injurious acts bring on. So, some Wee Gaggle questions:

- How long does it take us to speak harshly or uncharitably? How long does it take us to apologize? Why?
- What kind of things do we think to ourselves *before* we say, "I'm sorry" or "I overreacted"?
- What happens when we hear those words from someone we love?
- When I want to reject myself or others, I am learning to ...

This is a conversation ... if the theological pattern of calling for the preacher is the path of rising from the pew to enter the pulpit, the follower of Jesus must leave the pulpit to return to the pew, alongside others who have also come to see Jesus. This means that we live with the sermon not only as the people who "preach" but also as people who respond to the sermonic claim or idea. Wee gaggles exist at the intersection between pulpit and pew.

As for process, you have options. If you have more time, use a simple "circle talk" wherein each person has two or three minutes to share. Once a rhythm is established, ask someone else to moderate (keeping time). A talking stick or other symbol (pen, feather, chalice) helps everyone engage in careful speaking and prayerful listening. It is always okay to pass the "object" without speaking. If you have less time, you might want to ask questions of a small panel that elicit a feeling associated with a particular experience. People find a straightforward "yes" or "no" question (without elaboration) eases them into the problem so long as they're given a chance to briefly elaborate. Another easing approach is to use "I completely agree, I am neutral, I disagree" with a statement that is at the heart of the sermon. Always give people a chance to develop the "why" behind their "yes" or their "no" or their level of agreement or disagreement.

At another level, you might not want "answers" as such, but experiences, for example, "When I am welcomed, I feel [insert adjectives]"—depending on where it is in the service, it gives the congregation a chance to hear how one or two or three people are responding to the questions of the sermon. If it is appropriate, and with permission of the individuals involved, these insights can be part of a continuing congregational conversation with God's Word.

Wee Gaggles

Inflection Points: Calendar

Up on Old Rag Mountain on a high plateau of rock, near the Shenandoah National Park in Virginia, we could see a late afternoon thunderstorm building and moving toward us. We were overly exposed to lightning strikes. I decided to act quickly and move us out of harm's way before harm arrived. On another day, the heat and humidity hung over us like a wet towel. We made it about halfway before turning back. Weather changes our experience, doesn't it? One thing the calendar doesn't indicate is the weather—by that I mean, congregational energy or even your energy. We feel the electricity build towards Easter Day or a Pentecost or a Christmas Day service. Follow the lightning strike of God's resurrection action!

But sometimes, the air doesn't seem to be moving. During the yearly calendar, you will have Sundays where there just isn't a lot of heat in the room (body heat or institutional). I don't know if I'm alone in this, but I often find these Sundays are, ironically, some of the richest days for preaching. The Sunday after Christmas or Christ the King or some summer Sunday when most people are on holiday and the church is too, these often prove to be rich occasions. I don't quite know why. Is it because we're the "faithful few"? Or is it that the person who lives with the sermon is, by virtue of feeling less pressure, more able to speak to the congregation a word that lasts and lingers? Is it the text that is otherwise overshadowed by the "high days" of the Christian year? Maybe we should rename those "off-Sundays" as "Sunday Surprise." It's a bit like visiting with a litter of Border collies or finding a shark's tooth on the Brontë footpath. Surprises punctuate our experiences of the preaching journey. Off Sundays seem to offer gems of interest and insight. They surface something; maybe the unexpected visit of the Spirit. It flashes suddenly or sublimely. Those are unique gifts to the gathered community.

But I would go further: salvage those moments for other days in the church year, bring them back. Or (gasp!) preach a sermon twice. Don't do it dishonestly. Announce it. Proclaim it. And re-walk it—I sometimes think we enjoy our familiar treks simply because we know where the fun is going to be. My children, particularly when they were young, were less than enchanted by unfamiliar paths. However, as it became "our" walk, they bounded from one favorite spot to another—the old, abandoned schoolhouse of the Swiss Valley Park near Dubuque, or its suspension bridge, or the place where we would often sit on a bench in the winter, make snow angels, and drink hot cocoa. The kids looked forward to that spot—it was a "taste and see that the Lord is good" kind of moment. Reruns, or re-walks, speak to our fondness for the way beauty constantly renews itself.

We didn't talk about reruns in homiletics, did we? I know. I'm sorry. We were all enslaved by the idolatry of the original. I suspect that these so-called off-Sunday sermons reflect a distillation of our interpretive life. It is not the Easter sermon that you sweated for but the off-Sunday sermon that felt like a surprise—it's an easy "inflection point" and doesn't require anything from you but advance notice to the church—give them notice—you don't want people saying, "You've preached that sermon before!" They'll think you're cheating. Tell them in advance, tell them why (you like reruns, don't you?), and then do it. But not every Sunday.

Biblical Story: Beloved & Occasional Texts

My mom and I went to a nature preserve not far from where she lives in Sacramento, California. They live in the inner city of Sacramento. Gunshots, break-ins, and poverty exist all around. Mom has had a few scares over the years. She did not grow up in an urban setting but in the wilderness of Alaska. Today, she lives happily in the inner city, but still needs to find those life-giving spaces that only a river and wild nature provides. She took me to the Effie Yeaw (pronounced *yaw*) Nature Center, not far from where they live. While sitting on a bench near the American River, she said to me, "Do you know what we're doing? We're wilderness bathing." I thought, that's right, that's what this feels like.

In an increasingly intense preaching life, it feels right to be intentional about being in the presence of texts that "bathe" us or even "ravish" us with the love and promises of God. Lectionary or biblical patterns of preaching are all good, of course. But from time to time, we should bathe in the great stories of the Bible. Let me rattle off a few candidates for this category: Jeremiah's the potter's house; pray for the welfare of the city; Ezekiel's valley of dry bones; the stories of creation, Genesis 1:1–2:2 and 2:3 and on; the Beatitudes of Matthew 5:1–11; Matthew 28, or the Great Commission; or Romans 8, "nothing shall separate us from the love of God"; or Revelation, there shall neither be weeping nor suffering nor pain anymore (new creation); or the story of Joseph's reconciliation with his brothers; or Abraham and Sarah entertaining angels; or Psalms 139, 23, 121, 90, 42, 47, 133, 51; John's account of Jesus' dialogue with Nicodemus in chapter 3 (or equally significant the story of the Samaritan woman at the well); the raising of Lazarus; Ruth's pledge to be with Naomi; the story of the Emmaus walk; the "love chapter" of 1 Corinthians 13; the good Samaritan; the prodigal son.

In fact, if you are in possession of a book of common worship of whatever denominational flavor, and you were to look up texts associated with so-called "occasional services," you would find a selection of readings that resonate with our experience of God at threshold moments of life. Marriage, baptism, reaffirmation of faith, ordination, commissioning services, mission and ecology, justice and reconciliation, inter-religious and ecumenical services, healing and wholeness, death and resurrection—in some ways you could say that "occasional" is a misnomer, since each of these occasions is a kind of limit experience. As such, they often call on texts that speak in a limit way. There is no reason that you could not create a preaching plan around such powerfully evocative texts. Why not? Yes, they would be vista texts, well-worn and therein is the challenge. How do you see them freshly? But maybe that's overstated. As in a funeral, so also in a sermon that speaks from a foundational narrative of the Bible, it is about reconciling the great polarities of human experience: loneliness and community; death and resurrection; health and disease; alienation and reconciliation; and so on. I think it would be a shame if the only time we preached from Psalm 23 was when someone died. It is a powerful testimony to life. And it affords the person who lives with sermons an opportunity to read without apology the great classics of biblical theology.

Part Three: Community

Signposts for the Footpath

If you're new to a congregation, spend a couple of afternoons digging into the archives of the church, its sermons, bulletins, newsletters, and session minutes. These help you to see where the church has been as much as where it's going (or thinks it is going)—and perhaps the strategic and interpretive challenges you will inevitably face as you lead the congregation. Although you will have a lot to keep you busy in your first year, don't neglect this important process of excavation. The documents that church secretaries dutifully stow away in filing cabinets contain the memory of the congregation's footpath. It shows where they've been. Perhaps most importantly, it supplies clues for the how the church faced change: how did the congregation respond to change? Reject it? Accept it? Try to understand it? A healthy history of change will be evident in a congregation that seeks to understand change before exercising the executive function of accepting or rejecting (resisting) it. To that end, church archives contain artifacts, primary documents that record a decision to separate, terminate, dissolve, or unite. They reveal an ethos or stance relative to change over time.

As you go through these archival memories you will be learning the congregational DNA. Congregations cherish their memories—but they are not always scrutinized, which is tragic, particularly in a time when churches face fundamental challenges to their continued existence, at least some of it self-inflicted. The official publications of a church are often hagiographic rather than strictly historical—but just beneath the surface of these affectional narrations you will read more believable stories. The founding pastor of the last church I served was said to have been close friends with George Washington. The official and hagiographical accounts say that when Washington died, the founding minister died of heartbreak. In a conversation with member of the church, it turns out that it was probably suicide. Like this memory, some of the stories may be found in those who become the unofficial historians of the church, who separate the wheat from the chaff.

It is also helpful to see the history of the church as you consider the larger trends of national and regional movements within the country and denomination. A church with a long history has the advantage of having "been there"—a high steeple often includes a perception of its historic significance. But here, again, read closely. It is not that you're trying to strip the glossy varnish from the memory of the church, but as a pastoral leader you will need more than a passing acquaintance with the congregation's history as opposed to its hagiography. If congregations were as "welcoming" as they claim to be, we would be enjoying unrivalled church growth. The truth is that we are in the middle of a wide-scale decline.

A luncheon or evening series about the history of the church, and what it sees as its vital period (usually associated with a particularly influential pastorate), can be instrumental in forming a footpath of congregational reform. Although it is not technically a sermon, your careful reading of the historical documents of a church is a ministry that you are uniquely positioned to perform. There will be people in the church who know the history of that congregation better than you do, but they will not know that history in the *way* you do, as a pastoral theologian. As a pastor, you enjoy a unique place and a profound responsibility to sound out the depths of congregational consciousness. We join a congregation as people who walk alongside and who are entrusted with the work of interpretation of the journey of faith. Many of the people in the church you serve will only be superficially aware of the congregation's history—but that history exercises a profound influence over the behavior of the congregation. Only by excavating that memory in a priestly way can we move a community to initiate a reform of any substance—otherwise, congregations simply repeat the myths that served them well in another generation. It is not that we don't need myths, but we may need different myths for an hour such as this.

Chapter Eight

Difficult Journeys

"The way to right wrongs is to turn the light of truth upon them."

—Ida B. Wells

I've not yet had the experience of needing to call a mountain rescue team, but I've had a few moments where it became clear that going any farther, despite the dotted line, would be ill-advised. The inadvisability usually occurred to Rebecca before it did to me. My usual pattern is to say, "This looks complicated." Study it for a while. Then decide to carefully go forward, as far as I can, without endangering life and limb. Or turning back if that seems like the sensible thing to do—so far, I've been sensible.

Another difficult journey was the first time we attempted the Coast to Coast . . . while carrying our baby son, Gabriel, who was just about a year old and still nursing. For us, it seemed doable. We got the kit. I started going for neighborhood strolls with twenty pounds of weight on my back. I reduced everything that I would carry to an extreme minimum, as I would be carrying Gabriel. Apart from his ten or so pounds, most of the weight I was carrying was taken up by diapers, baby food, wipes, and other baby things. I still thought, "This is doable."

Difficult Journeys

But it wasn't very long into the walk that we concluded that we had been mistaken. Early on, an old back injury flared up and began sending snakes of pain between my shoulder blades. For a time, I was simply blind with pain. We stopped in a barley field. But I wasn't in a barley field, not really. I was in a cloud of pain, and I could only remember what we would do in the Army after a long hike with forty-pound rucksacks—we'd drop our bags off our shoulders and onto the ground. Which is precisely what I did with the carrier holding Gabriel. I only realized what I'd done after I heard him wailing. Fortunately, there was no lasting harm (not that we know of), but it was the beginning of the end of that journey. We (or rather my other half) also discovered how difficult it is to nurse on the side of a Lake District peak, with the wind howling and rain spitting. We called it off in Grasmere and booked a holiday house in Wales.

In the life of preaching, it may not be that the path ahead was too difficult but rather we chose a path that was too easy. Or as G. K. Chesterton says, "Christianity was not tried and found difficult but it was found difficult and not tried."

Does Chesterton's statement apply to those of us who live with sermons? Do we feel sometimes the tug of controversy and deliberately and habitually kick that to the prayers of the people, not because we're wise but because we're frightened? If fear is a natural thing, and I think it is, what remedies exist for our fear of undertaking the difficult sermon? This chapter makes a case for difficult preaching—not because we need to make preaching difficult but because it is difficult whether we make it that way or not. Of course, the difficulty of the gospel, the stumbling block, is not identical with our self-inflicted errors. How can we preach the difficult sermon so that the difficulty is in the gospel rather than our fumbling? This chapter gives shape and practical suggestions for the repair or rescue of the preaching life from either superficial optimism on one side or merely being unhelpfully difficult on the other side. We want, in the name of the gospel, to learn to be difficult for the right reasons and not the wrong ones.

Preaching to Deconstruct Whiteness

Some of us will remember the saying of Origen relative to our preaching: "Comfort the afflicted and afflict the comfortable." Does it almost sound as if he's admitting that perhaps he got it wrong a time or two, that sometimes his preaching afflicted the afflicted and comforted the comfortable?

Part Three: Community

Our task in preaching has never been easy. Yet today feels different, doesn't it? We get it in this "I can't breathe"–"Me Too" world. Lives are at stake. Church teaching has valorized the pain and suffering of Jesus with deleterious effects on those who are most vulnerable to domestic abuse; those who live with a sexuality that is not in agreement with the norms or at least not settled into the norm can and do feel profoundly rejected; those who live with the legacies of slavery, genocide, and politically and racially motivated violence and at the same time endure the church's silence and sometimes its complicity; a former US president boasts about sexual assault against women and White Christian nationalists celebrate by mobilizing for his election campaign; the aftermath of the Supreme Court's overturning of *Roe vs. Wade* is like a slow-moving bomb, as state legislatures roll out legislation to regulate women's bodies; the fragility and complexity of adolescence has always been complicated and is even more so now, and yet preachers are guilty of using this age group as the butt of their pulpit jokes, hardly indicating welcome and much less speaking to a crisis of hope in this generation. Consider also those who have experienced a past trauma which continues to haunt their daily existence—they may cry out for a word from the pulpit, but they also may flee from it remembering all too clearly how they have been re-traumatized by clumsy attempts to care.

How do we make right that sacred relationship between our speaking and our vocation of justice and healing?

During a conference gathering around the topic of the legacies of slavery, a White minister demanded that a room full of mostly White ministers answer this question: "Why don't we preach against White privilege and structural racism?" A complicated answer must surely follow.

Today, those who live with the sermon in its cultural context cannot, with integrity, ignore the legacies of White supremacy. To live in this age is to live with in a spirit of agitated intelligence and activated faith. We're not talking about mere apology, and certainly not a transaction as such, but righting a relationship that has been fundamentally abused and then either ignored outright or minimized. Jesus' teaching on the commandments that go to the obligation to maintain right relationships is unsparing:

> You have heard that it was said to those of ancient times, "You shall not murder"; and "whoever murders shall be liable to judgment." But I say to you that if you are angry with a brother or sister, you will be liable to judgment; and if you insult a brother or sister, you will be liable to the council; and if you say, "You fool," you will be

liable to the hell of fire. So when you are offering your gift at the altar, if you remember that your brother or sister has something against you, leave your gift there before the altar and go; first be reconciled to your brother or sister, and then come and offer your gift. Come to terms quickly with your accuser while you are on the way to court with him, or your accuser may hand you over to the judge, and the judge to the guard, and you will be thrown into prison. Truly I tell you, you will never get out until you have paid the last penny. (Matt 5:21–26)

Many interpreters take Matthew's antitheses between the ethical requirements of the law (thesis) and the "but I say to you" (antithesis) of Jesus as a theory of replacement. Eric Barreto's commentary on this text from Matthew corrects traditional theories of replacement by underlining the key place of relationships in Jesus' ethics:

> What if broken relationships among neighbors, family, and friends are not just social obstacles among us but a barometer for our relationship to God too? What if the obverse of murder is not just avoiding killing but reparative reconciliation? . . . . Relationality is itself a way to draw near to the God who calls us to righteousness.[1]

Black and other people of color have lived with and suffered under the seemingly "invisible" White gospel that allowed discrimination and violence against their bodies, literally "replacing" cultures of color with norms of whiteness.

White preachers have something to do with that.

How is it possible to preach as if whiteness doesn't exist among White people? Do we stop church, a kind of literal intervention, and call a congregational meeting where the single agenda item is to go and begin the journey of reconciliation? Or bring one sermon on Racial Justice Sunday or, "dodge that bullet" by migrating the "concern" to prayers? Or do we, with our communities of faith, adopt a season of preaching repair to those human relationships?

What we need to think about is the place of difficult repair. Trigger warnings are a relatively new phenomenon in preaching—but the phenomenon of trauma has been with us for a long time, albeit ignored or trivialized. The twenty-first century, according to Jürgen Moltmann, is full of blood yet our preaching feels chirpy. In 1979 the Black comedian Richard Pryor did a stand-up routine and told how police use excessive force

---

1. Barreto, "Commentary on Matthew 5:21–37," para. 7.

and extrajudicial killings as a normal form of policing the Black body.[2] The audience appeared to be mostly White. Black people, according to Pryor, know this biting satire as a profound form of lament on a scale mostly undetected by the White ticket holders.

Pryor challenges those of us who would preach to undertake this difficult journey—and trigger warnings play a role. As a concept, triggers come from the mental health field, but they are widely used in classrooms and increasingly in sermons. The American Psychology Association defines a trigger as "a stimulus that elicits a reaction. For example, an event could be a trigger for a traumatic memory and an accompanying state of emotional arousal."[3] Katharine Ponte, who self-describes as a person who is "happily living in recovery from severe bipolar 1 disorder," says that a trigger is something that elicits physical symptoms (sweating, heavy breathing) and/or emotional reactions (I am being attacked, I feel unloved). Once triggered, they might lack insight into why they are feeling the way they are, not being able to draw a line between a memory and this state of emotional upset. Telling them that they're "too sensitive" or behaving "irrationally" only makes matters worse.[4]

Educators deliver insight to our problem because, like a church, a classroom is a learning environment. A university classroom serves as a relatively safe place for difficult topics. Difficult subjects may not be surprising for a classroom, but that familiarity does not mitigate against resurfacing trauma. Meredith Logan, who teaches classes on sexual violence, law, and justice, credits the humble trigger with giving her students the space in which to learn: "My experience is that if you give students that space and you give them that information, they absolutely rise to the occasion." Her syllabus includes this trigger warning:

> This course is about sexual violence. We will be discussing rape and other forms of sexual abuse in class and you are expected to complete assignments concerning these topics. Some of the readings and films for this course are graphic and include narrative, testimony, and descriptions of sexual violence.

At a minimum, a trigger warning explicitly acknowledges past trauma and, symbolically, implicitly names an obligation to preach on difficult topics.

---

2. See Richard Pryor (1979) at https://www.youtube.com/watch?v=ZWulvchFpYs.
3. American Psychological Association, "Trigger."
4. Ponte, "Understanding Mental Illness Triggers," paras. 1–5.

Difficult Journeys

Sometimes we hear that the sermon should barely touch on difficult issues or if it does, we are asked to make those so vague as to be almost undetectable—in the end, we conclude that we don't need warnings because the gospel is two miles wide but only two inches deep. Others might object to trigger warnings as a form of helicopter homiletics, overly protective. My first reaction when I heard about the trigger warning was along these lines, that this was overly protective. But after witnessing firsthand the physical and emotional toll of someone experiencing a trigger, in my mind, there's no debate. If a trigger warning gives someone space to exercise self-care, why wouldn't I do that? I also suspect that the real objection of those who dislike the concept of a "trigger warning" is not based on an objection to "trigger warnings" as such, but to the difficult sermon, full stop. A trigger warning acts as a symbol, not unlike the cross, signifying the Spirit's power to take us from death to life and to do so with grace and gentleness.

A stronger objection to the difficult sermon is that if it is all confrontation (telling it like it is, the pulpit being the original source of God's indignation), we may only "succeed" in creating allies and opposition parties, while producing very little learning. This is probably the single largest and best reason ministers choose to avoid difficult topics in preaching. But if we knew of another way, would we take it? Is it possible to preach difficult sermons in an environment that fosters learning and human formation? What if there were a way to preach on difficult topics that didn't result in a zero-sum game? Are there meaningful ways of navigating difficult topics so that people grow in the gospel?

What I'm pondering here in the idea of the trigger is really a theology of reconciliation or a theology of human repair. The seeming novelty of the trigger warning implicitly acknowledges that the church has not spoken when it should have. It acknowledges generational failure to afflict the comfortable. Apology seems to be everywhere and nowhere, as in, "If I've ever offended you, I apologize"—it means nothing and it returns to nothing. Or the apologies that now get texted out after some celebrity says or does something that retraumatizes whole segments of the population, but it was done on the advice of their legal counsel. I'm not talking about "apologies" that check the box. No. This is not what we're about. The word that we're looking for is reconciliation or reparations or repair. Or the difficult preaching that leads to the path of reconciliation in the name of the whole human being.

Part Three: Community

Repair for the Split in Two

Returning to the initial question, "Why don't White preachers preach against structural racism?": A clue might be in the story of the "split" pair of Tsimshian masks. In 1879, one half of this mask, with open apertures for eyes, was shipped (through missionary cooperation with European imperialism) from British Columbia to the Paris Musée de l'Homme—in the 1970s, during an exhibition, the sighted mask "traveled" to Canada, where its other half, unsighted, was "discovered":

> [The] mask, without apertures for eyes, fits snugly over the Paris [sic] mask, with its round eyeholes. It is thought that the pair was worn in a *naxnox* performance, where an individual's personal power was displayed in dance. To present the illusion of the eyes opening and closing, the dancer must have turned quickly while removing the "blind" mask to reveal the one with eyeholes. The dancer would have needed considerable strength to hold the four-kilogram inner "sighted" mask in place with the wooden mouthpiece, although a harness attached through holes in the mask's rim might have helped support it. The "unsighted" mask may have been held in the hand, concealed by the dancer's costume.[5]

What if the story of this bifurcated mask could operate as a parable for the hermeneutic of whiteness, which is only "sighted" and seldom consciously aware of its blindness? Does the colonial missionary imperialism of yesterday and today's White Christian nationalism show symptoms of an advanced form of theo-psycho schizoid mentality, a term coined by Black British theologian Anthony Reddie?[6] This mental health condition manifests itself in part as a denial of the sociopolitical reality of White skin while at the same time advancing the politics of White identity. At a biological level, the color of one's skin may mean next to nothing, but sociologists

---

5. "Tsimshian Mask" in Canadian Museum of History (no author, no date), paras. 1–2.

6. Reddie is speaking about the unreconstructed notions of whiteness in some parts of the Black majority Pentecostal churches. Reddie, *Theologising Brexit*, 43.

predict its impact on all sorts of measures—income, neighborhood, voting patterns, and so much more. Is naivete also at play in the phenomenon of colonial amnesia—the tendency to forget or minimize the violence of the colonial missionary empire? Is this a symptom a of a split theo-psycho personality? If this is the diagnosis, what is the medicine? How might the White person come to be clothed and in their right mind, rather than raging in the graveyard of delusional whiteness?

Mark's story of the Gerasene demoniac suggest itself as a lens for thinking about the delusional power of whiteness. Being possessed by Legion, we know that the demoniac isn't under the power of merely "spiritual" powers but socio-economic and imperial powers. A report that a Roman legion was on its way would strike terror in an oppressed population like Mark's. Legion represents the shock and awe of Rome. Yet in this story, a Roman legion is reduced to begging to be housed in the skins of pigs and then, shortly after, self-annihilating in a disorderly scramble over the edge of a cliff. Jesus demonstrates the futility of coercive Roman power. However, before Jesus confronts and names the issue as Legion, the person with the infection of legion-power is seen to be uncontrollable and delusional, living among the dead. At the end of the story, the sight of the person "clothed and in his right mind" stuns the village, as in they had not imagined that the "torn" identity could ever be restored, or even what "restored" might look like. We see a picture of the repair of the split personality.

How do we, as preachers, perform this kind of repair? First, we need to acknowledge that the rupture in the human condition is far too vast for any one person or preacher to navigate. At the height of the MeToo movement, how many male pastors felt the double pang of inadequacy and wanting to speak into that moment? That may be where a preacher starts, with *his* inadequacy. Naming our limitations begins a fair and reasonable dialogue—not only for MeToo but for the massive social issues of our day. We are seldom experts and even if we were that expertise is not the basis for our interpreting. Our limitations, a natural boundary, may inform a trigger warning: there are no experts in the room, least of all the person in the pulpit. In the pulpit, we acknowledge our limitations as an interpreter; humility helps in forming trust and transparency, and it gives everyone a place to start.

We also need to simply get over ourselves as the "primary" preacher who alone is "ordained" to interpret Scripture for this hour. Yes, as pastor, you are preaching most Sundays, but it makes complete pastoral and homiletic sense to invite different voices and perspectives (for example, a professor who teaches about sexual violence with wisdom and sensitivity) into the Sunday service on difficult topics that require something like expertise in the social sciences. Think about the community that you walk with, both on Sunday and beyond. Who is in that community that could bring a voice of wisdom or expertise or empathic connection to that setting? The traditional Service of the Word will survive, and it may do more than that—it may support a congregation as it gets acquainted with itself as a place that meets life as it is and yet does so in the spirit of a student who rises to the occasion, or who meets the costliness of the gospel, clothed and in its right mind. It may also renew its commitment to true and substantial hospitality to those who live in the shadows of the "mostly healthy" delusion of American Christianity.

As people who lead worship, most of us tap into educational modes of communicating. Whether anyone can teach someone else "how to be antiracist" is debatable; however, it is possible for us to learn. Difficult topics call on more inclusive forms of learning . . . and not less than a good sermon. This means we acknowledge the limitation of a Sunday sermon. It goes so far. Some topics ask us not just to listen or to be instructed but to be transformed by the renewal of our minds. Reddie speaks of the role of participative Black liberation theology as "[a form of] Black theology that arises from the creative and playful engagement of ordinary people taking part in exercises and drama, in which, through their shared learning and reflection, new insights that relate to Black theology are able to emerge." The "play" equips us to become "changed agents" because of an encounter with Black theology.[7] We don't learn, Reddie argues, by simply listening to the "right" ideas in a sermon or in a lecture, even with a trigger warning. Nor are we particularly susceptible to learning when we're feeling stressed or exposed. Forms of play—activities like drama, games, and exercises in a safer space—reveal potential space for genuine encounter, self-discovery, and transformation.

One of the exercises designed by Reddie helps participants achieve what he calls their "complex subjectivity" as opposed to the "fixed identity," which is ascribed by norms of whiteness. According to Reddie, ideologies of whiteness, which is distinct from White people, ascribe to White people all kinds of virtues, privileges, and forms of superiority. The fixed identity of whiteness enforces whiteness as a norm for all people. White people are

---

7. Reddie, *Is God Color Blind?*, xiv.

Difficult Journeys

not identical with whiteness, but they are perhaps more susceptible to its seductive power than people of color. That is, they don't know the depth of their own sickness. Allegiance to deforming whiteness becomes a slogan rather than a soul. It is not that everything about White people is bad, he says. There is much to be celebrated. However, when White people cannot see themselves as complex human beings, belonging to a whole rainbow of human experience, that introduces a profound schism into what it means to be a White person. This is something that people of color know from their earliest years, but that White people are at risk of never knowing from their earliest (or later) years.

That's the purpose of the circle exercise, as it helps participants "see" their intrinsic complexity (White or Black).[8] It also exposes concepts of whiteness (neutrality, invisibility, being the center, purity) as they disguise or limit our self-understanding. As a relatively simple exercise it feels safe and somewhat playful. The picture below is of my own work in the identity exercise that I undertook with a group of United Reformed Church people near Blackburn.

Reddie tells the facilitator that when they introduce the exercise, they should not give away too much, that it is a way of naming the often-unnamed power of whiteness (and gender constructions). If we give away too much, the exercise loses its disclosive impact. The inner circle, he says, is that which is most core to our identity. No more than two terms that define us. There are no wrong answers. Given that we'd been talking about whiteness for the previous forty-five minutes, that the trigger warning I gave at the beginning of the session included the topic of the session (structural racism and the legacies of slavery and concepts of whiteness) it seemed as if I'd "given away too much" already. Everyone, I thought, would "guess" that if their race was White or that since race and concepts of whiteness had been subject number one in our conversation, this would feature in the inner circle or at least one of the circles.

---

8. Reddie, *Is God Color Blind?*, 39–43.

Part Three: Community

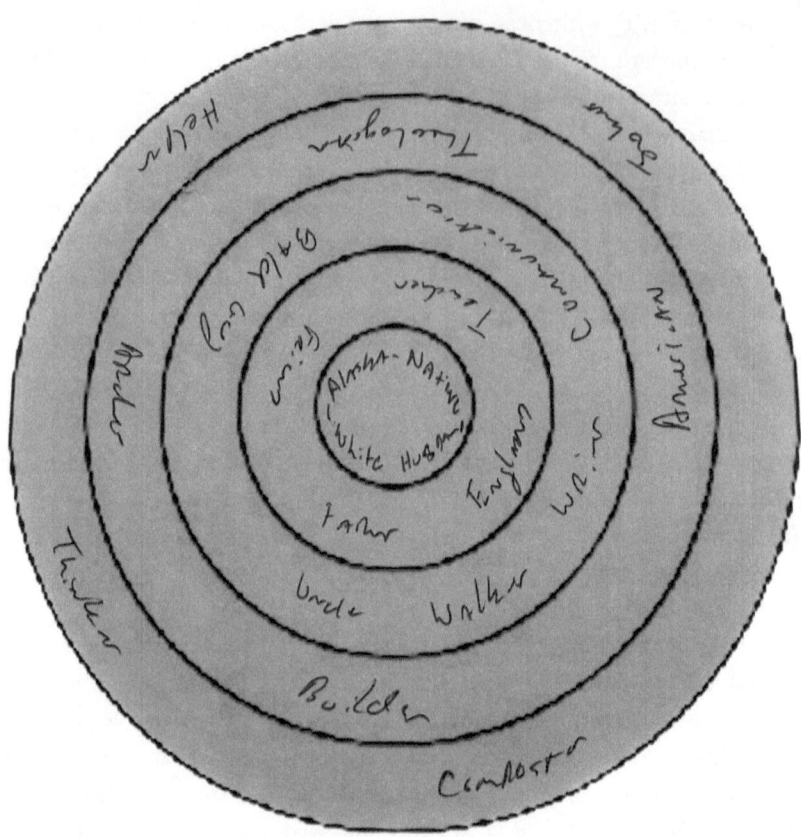

After filling out our circles, we set those to one side, with the promise that we could come back to them. We listened to Reddie talk about achieving "complex subjectivity" and what that looks like for White people.[9] Then I asked the group to break into pairs and look at their circles with the following questions: is there anything you would change after hearing the podcast with Reddie? Is there any delusion within whiteness that is dangerous and needs to be named? How might White people join as happily visible members of the rainbow of human identity?

After listening to Reddie, and talking again about complex subjectivity, I asked whether anyone felt the need to change anything in their identity circle. People looked blankly at one another and at me. I asked if anyone put down that they were White (most of the group was White); again, no one raised their hand. One person admits that they didn't even think about

9. Hoch, "Podcast with Dr Anthony Reddie."

Difficult Journeys

it, meaning the color of their skin. Then something happens. A crack of consciousness appears: "I didn't say that I'm a woman, either." A quietness slips over the room. How is it possible that a woman could suppress her gender? How is it that we fail to see in ourselves what sociological studies can simply tell from voting patterns, earnings, educational attainment, neighborhoods—that being White or being a woman is not invisible but a real sociological and empirical fact with decisive implications for how we live? And how is it that after nearly an hour of talk about concepts of whiteness, when it came to this exercise, not a single White person included their racial identity in any of the circles?

It wasn't that they were not engaged. Before the exercise, this group was nodding, and seemingly following the concepts of whiteness, but when it came to this exercise it felt almost as if the talk of the previous hour had vanished. That is, until it reappeared and suddenly it was a different kind of space. Maybe it is like the discovery that two masks, one all seeing and the other never seeing, belong together—and click, suddenly, without quite knowing that we were deranged a moment ago, we were clothed and in our right minds.

Bringing these two back together may feel like a healing, like the "sighted" part of the mask being reunited with the unsighted mask, the "missing" half. Liberation theologies may be seen as the repair of the alienation of our anthropology. Black liberation theology, according to Reddie, is a challenge but it is also a gospel of healing, first for Black people and secondarily, if they are willing to receive it, for White people. Black and Red theologies deconstruct ideologies of whiteness because these ideologies ascribe delusional superiority to White people and inferiority to people of color. Intentionally intersectional theologies, from mixed race people, are also a part of the healing. Part of healing is naming the good that White people bring to the world but also renouncing the bad things—the privilege, the fragility, the delusional superiority. But you can't do any of that until you learn its power in your own way. Play, drama, and creative exercises foster a safer space for personal interrogation and change. The other part of the healing is restoration, bringing White people into the rainbow of the human being—to be a White person is to be a part of a complex whole.

To recover that kind of complexity, our storytelling needs to go after the complexity of every person, particularly our heroes. Begin with Jesus, or specifically Jesus and the Syrophoenician woman of Mark 7:24–30. In this story, the woman demonstrates that maybe Jesus isn't exactly "clothed and in his right mind"—by contrast, she is clothed and in her right mind. She proves to be a shrewd theological debater and, in fact, is the only person in Mark who outwits Jesus in debate about the character of God. By the end of this encounter, Jesus sees the world and this unlikely interlocutor in a different light. Or maybe he simply sees her, and the world God so loves, whereas before he did not see her or know her. Notably, Jesus does not commend her for her religious faith (as he does in Matthew) but for what she *says*—in other words, because what she says agrees with what is true and just and Jesus assents to that truth. Is Jesus any less God because he can learn from a Syrophoenician woman? Or is he a God worthy of the name precisely because he can learn from a woman?

Empire has always been about raising the flag, perfecting the imperial program, ultimately engaging in omnicide, the killing of everything in the name of the perfect, an idol—and yet these "perfect" ideals do not see, hear, or speak. Only real human beings or the Real Human Being sees, hears, and speaks.

Signposts for the Footpath

A sign you'll see posted in England around lakes reads: "Warning Deep Water/Do Not Swim"—it seems typically English to worry people about nothing. As in, if you swim in a lake, it's usually because the water is deep, as in you can't touch the bottom. Maybe that's somewhat how people feel about preaching, as if why warn anyone about anything? Wiser souls remind us that sermons can and sometimes do lead us into something like a catacomb of emotions, isolation, alienation, injustice, and despair—but do we know how to leave the catacombs, or do we become its captives, a resurrection indefinitely deferred? We know that risk exists. If there ever was a day when a sermon contained within it unseen hazards, just beneath what otherwise seems like calm, still waters, it is our day.

Maybe a trigger warning would be well-advised. There was, for example, that time when I compared a traditionally White and liberal church's attitude towards its endowment (which it wanted to preserve at all costs) with those

Difficult Journeys

defending Confederate statues. It was around the time that these statues were being toppled in Richmond and in Baltimore. I thought I was being careful when I asked, "Is our desire to preserve the endowment analogous to those who want to keep the Confederate statues?" It was well-known, but not said too loudly, that the endowment was financed by people in the church's history who got their wealth from financing the slave trade. This analogy was inspiring for some while for others it seemed to be triggering. I thought to myself, "How did I not see this coming?" I hadn't experienced "White fragility" until it stung me that Sunday afternoon.

Would a trigger have helped? I don't know but if I had to do it again, I would include a trigger warning that named the phenomenon of White fragility, that some of what I was going to say that morning might not be easy to hear. While I am not sure that you can preach a gospel that is related to Jesus of Nazareth and not piss some people off, a trigger warning may give people the space to choose to go to those places and, at the same time, implicitly remind everyone that the gospel includes a stumbling block. We can in "gospel" conscience prepare people who want that message. No one is "watering" down anything. I'm talking about creating living space whereby our listeners have a human chance of learning. What is more, while hazards do lurk in the preaching moment, sometimes our errors are self-inflicted. This is the preacher who is to be commended for their courage but not their common sense. I'm speaking of myself, of course!

David Benjamin Blower, a poet, singer, and self-described post-evangelical, relates an experience of a friend of his who was reading a book in a café—it serves as a metaphor for the value of margins and how the rhetoric of today seems to narrow them or, alternately, exclude them. Blower tells how an elderly person sidled up to his friend while she was reading: "Have you noticed," the elderly stranger asked, "how the margins on books have gotten smaller?" Without any further explanation she ambled off, leaving David's friend with that enigmatic observation. David's reflection on the margins impresses me as relevant to those who aim to preach in difficult times:

> That metaphor [of the shrinking margins] became important to her . . . the sense in which the space around the edges of the body of the text that has its thing to say used to be much bigger, people used to make notes in it and put their own thoughts around it, in some sort of Talmudic fashion. But over time the margins get smaller and smaller, and the main message becomes the thing that dominates and there isn't space for much else.

Part Three: Community

Have our margins in the sermon gotten too narrow? Does the congregation participate in this difficult journey? One of the gifts that preachers can offer to repair our public space is to preserve those margins, acknowledge space that rightly exists for our own thinking and being.

David also mines this image in another direction, considering this so-called "blank space" as space that may find its voice, may be heard:

> I see a paradox these days in that there's cultural and political reactionary energies that are almost wholly motivated by the anxiety that the margins are getting bigger, margins are spilling over, draining our welfare system . . . the margins are about to sink the boat . . . the character of the tensions between the margins and the main story . . . feels like it's at some kind of turning point or crisis.[10]

In this surprising shift of view, the margins are not so much "blank space" but peopled spaces. What would it be like to think in terms of peopled margins, places of hospitality, people living with trauma, in the sermonic moment? What might be a path for naming significant experiences of trauma within a community of faith?

During a session for churches on facing change and stressful situations, Hein ten Cate, a clinical psychologist who specializes in trauma, reports that when something triggers an emotional reaction, it's often tapping into a "state persistent memory"—an experience that was not processed or digested and just sits there, waiting to be triggered. When it is triggered, it as if the person were undergoing the experience again in real time and in a totally different context. The event may be a decade old and, for the most part, may be invisible (just beneath the surface). However, if triggered by a vivid account or an account that they aren't prepared for (and thus do not have the opportunity to care for themselves), that trigger can send a human person reeling into a place that you don't want to go. You, the preacher, may be courageous, but at whose expense? Let it be your practice to go gently when speaking of human trauma.

The clinical psychologist who I mentioned above modeled good practice while working with a large group of church leaders on how to cope with difficult experiences. First, he gave a general warning, a "trigger" warning: "We're going to talk about something that might trigger difficult memories. If that's you, please care for yourself. If you need to step away to get a glass of water, it's okay to do that." Tone and content conveyed authentic caring for spaces that we might not see and spaces in ourselves that we might

---

10. Blower and Postlethwaite, "Changed by the Margins" (episode 5).

not acknowledge unless given permission to do so. The second signpost opened the door a little further, so that we could see what was coming and whether we could cope . . . or not: "I'm going to describe an accident. It's not a real accident. It's hypothetical. And, importantly, no one gets hurt. Shaken, but not hurt. Upset but not injured." Then he proceeded to talk about a hypothetical driver, driving through a hypothetical intersection, colliding with a hypothetical bicyclist. "No one is injured," he repeats, "but just shaken up. There's no anger, either. Bicyclist is shaken up and you are, too." Then he asks, "What are you feeling right now?"

He asked for one person who would feel comfortable talking through these feelings. A woman raised her hand. "What," he asked her, "would you do with those feelings afterwards, when you got to your office? Would you tell people what happened? Or would you want to process it? Who would you call? When? How would you sleep that night? Would this experience color your next experience with a bicyclist, and if so, how?" Then he changed the question. "Let's say the same accident happens. Again, no injuries. Nobody goes to the hospital, but this time the bicyclist is very angry at you. Accusatory. Abusive." And then the same line of questions. But this time the woman spoke of "going into herself" and feelings of vulnerability and perhaps shame, not wanting to be exposed to her workmates.

Oddly enough, I was the sole bicyclist in the group. I had been thinking of this the whole time. I wasn't particularly happy to be described as the person who gets hit by a car or the person who becomes angry at a careless driver. Only a month earlier, I had a near collision with a car that could have been quite bad, and mostly for me. As it happened, we both quickly admitted fault (I was going too fast down the hill, and she was going too fast up the hill); I was shaken; the driver was shaken; but we were both grateful that there was no serious damage.

I wasn't overpowered by the descriptions of the accident, though part of me still felt it nipping at the edges of memory. The trigger warning and the margins allowed me to access this difficult topic in a way that felt safer than I might have expected. If that was true for me, feeling quite vulnerable, others probably felt that capacity in themselves—perhaps there is a lesson for preachers as well.

Chapter Nine

Distance Walking

"This is what we are about: We plant seeds that one day will grow. We water seeds already planted, knowing that they hold future promise... We cannot do everything and there is a sense of liberation in realizing that. This enables us to do something and to do it well. It may be incomplete, but it is a beginning, a step along the way, an opportunity for the Lord's grace to enter and do the rest. We may never see the end results, but that is the difference between the master builder and the worker. We are workers, not master builders; ministers, not messiahs. We are prophets of a future not our own."

—Oscar Romero

As I was preparing to walk the Camino, I was given a backpack by a member of my family. It was not an "ergonomically" designed backpack, the sort that they make today. It wasn't designed with the hiker in mind—it was for hauling equipment from an airboat to an Alaskan hunting camp. If they left the camp, they didn't carry this pack, or at least not far—from the banks of the Tanana River to the cabin. Most of their "stuff" they threw into the airboat and the "hike" was the ride on the river. The backpack was purely for carrying bulky items a short distance. By contrast, I belonged to this pack for the five-hundred-mile walk of the Camino de Santiago. It was a

Distance Walking

rude pack, ugly, utilitarian. One of the steel bands of its frame was bent, so that it cut into my back as I walked.

Why did I take this pack? It was free and I was a graduate student at the time. That, however, doesn't explain what I put in it: camping-style pots and pans (cafés line the path and most days I was able to get a cappuccino with ease), a couple of very thick volumes, including a French dictionary (I was studying for a French exam that I was to take in the autumn), a pair of running shoes (why did I think I needed running shoes on a five-hundred-mile walk?), a heavy Nikon camera (I carried that behemoth, including a massive telephoto lens, crazy), and too many changes of clothing. At the time, that seemed like good packing. Until the Pyrenees Mountains happened—and they nearly put me out of the Camino on day two of the walk. I might not have been carrying too much in relative terms, but given the climb, I felt every ounce. And water. It's so important to stay hydrated and, of course, I didn't. It wasn't that I was ignoring water needs. I drank my two cannisters of water before I reached the summit. And then my muscles started to cramp. I put on a brave face as other pilgrims continued up and over the Pyrenees.

Looking back, I wonder why I resisted asking for help. Pride? Male ego? Shame? Probably all of the above. The good news is that I found a water supply just near the top of the Pyrenees and I made it—or I walked the fifteen or sixteen miles for that day, and I still had hundreds of miles to go. I was in physical agony. An old back injury was telling me it wasn't too happy about the weight; I had acquired painful blisters. I had a decision to make, and it came down to the straightforward question: if I continued like this, would I make it? I had my doubts. I'd heard stories about people who went home because of injuries, including tendonitis. My body whimpered in protest. I listened. I gave up my itinerary, found a hotel short of my planned stop, and packed it in. It felt like cheating, but I booked two nights, got something to eat, and then slept for the rest of the day.

The day before I checked out, I laid everything I had in my possession on my bed, and I reduced. I went from five T-shirts to two, a clean one in the pack and one to wear during the day; same for pants (got rid of the blue jeans, too heavy); socks were similarly reduced; I was not camping or preparing my own meals, so the camping kit that I had purchased in New Jersey had to go. I remember looking a bit mournfully at everything that I had stacked on the bed as I walked out the door—but my body thanked me.

Part Three: Community

I made the decision to complete the walk and to do that I needed to reduce the burden on my back. But note that what I bore was not only the physical burden—people who undertake the Camino often feel cares that are not seen but are felt no less and perhaps weigh more on the pilgrim than either miles or physical burden. I was no different. While I was still in Paris, I wandered through a square dedicated to an exhibit for the human journey. One sculpture, *Le Pelerin*, was in a minimalist style, showing a human figure bent double under a massive weight. Those cares, whatever their form, would require tenderness while the other called on a calculated approach to weight management.

When I set out on the Camino, I started alone. One of the questions you get asked on the Camino, is, "Are you solo or with a group?" My answer was always solo but what solo meant changed with the walk. Within the first week I fell into a group—a group of people who each answered that question the same way I did. Over time, we began to be known as the "Solos" to other groups up and down the Camino. There were about six of us, each of us coming to the path from different nationalities and life experiences. Yet, however different, we shared meals, helped one another with blisters and bandages, came to understand each other's need for community as well as solitude.

This leads me to think that the tenderness of soul care amid the challenges of vocational journey is as important as planning themes and working with the musician. This problematic exists for people who live with the sermon—we organize, plan, and conceive an idea for the season of preaching. When we think about living with more than one sermon and indeed with the preaching life writ large, the practical matter of organizing or planning for preaching comes together with the deeper problem of our unique ways of carrying this burden. In this chapter, we explore the problem of the sermon as day hike or sprint versus living with the sermon which recalls a long-distance pilgrimage where planning figures into the successful completion of the walk. In the spirit of the care of the preacher, we think about the person who can look on our work and us with one degree of separation from our life and community, that is, the role of a mentor or counselor. Once upon a time, when the church had more ministers than it does today, it was natural to find a minister, often older or perhaps in another denomination, who could help you reflect on your journey. Today, we speak of coaches, mentors, spiritual guides, or pastoral supervisors. Those of us who live with the sermon need the distance and the experience of a counselor, who can help us when we need help and challenge us when we need challenging. They're not walking the same path but ideally they have walked an analogous path. We will also name the problem of the perfect sermon or the monumentalism that sometimes haunts those who preach—acceptance of people, things, and circumstances extends to the sermon and our way of looking over the breadth of our work.

Long Distance Preaching

We learn to preach almost like sprinters . . . or maybe we prepare our sermons like sprinters. That's not all bad. Classes in seminary focus on the basics of preaching, including the exegetical process, organization, delivery, and critical reflection on a sermon given in class and congregational settings. Assessment skews towards Exhibit One, the sermon, rather than to the preaching life. For this, we assigned a book like Barbara Brown Taylor's *The Preaching Life* and students enjoyed her work. However, it existed on one end of the spectrum, where the art of being and the art of doing were almost alien to one another. Taylor gave us an inspiring vision for the preacher but often students sweated through the required preaching assignments. In seminary, as we juggled classes and family life, maybe the sermon felt like a last minute fifty-yard dash. My students didn't always believe me, but the fact is that sometimes you find yourself composing a sermon literally as you go to the church, perhaps even adapting or revising while you're in the pulpit.

While in PhD studies, I was pastoring a church part-time. I'd like to tell you that I spent an hour for every minute in the pulpit. I didn't. Not even close. One Sunday morning, on the way to services, I literally pulled off the road into a cemetery where, for about five or ten minutes, I simply walked from tombstone to tombstone. I made a few notes—an epitaph here and an epitaph there, a person who died too young, another who never really lived. I "composed" the rest of the sermon in the twenty minutes it took me to drive to the church. It wasn't a model representation of how one continues in this vocation for the long haul. Maybe it was a sermon that I should be ashamed to talk about. But it is also true that sometimes a week or two weeks in ministry simply knocks you off your feet. There will be times like that and then and there you need to be able to prepare quickly for Sunday.

But that's the exception that proves the rule. Too many of us in the pulpit are lulled into the habit of the exceptional "sprint" and the preaching office suffers as a result. You can't sprint vocation. The weird and ironic thing is that in the sprint view, the sermon is the most important thing (we suddenly become wretched with intensity) and least important thing (we left it to the last minute). We think that we care about the life of preaching but in fact what we care about is getting through Sunday. If we think that everything boils down to the sermon on Sunday, that it's the "finish line," have we missed something important? Did we sign up for the sprint or for the lifetime of preaching?

Think of a day-hiker. Ironically, day-hikers don't plan very far ahead but they carry a lot of equipment, much of it masking the nature of preaching itself, which is ongoing digest. By contrast, in the long journey, you evolve into a minimalist; you learn exactly what you need, and you jettison what you don't. The Appalachian Trail includes both day-hikers and through-hikers, people undertaking the entire 2,100 miles. How do you tell an Appalachian through-hiker from a day-hiker? It's easy. You don't even need to ask. The through-hiker smells. I'm not saying that preachers (or through-hikers) all smell bad. Some do. What is true for all of us is that, over time, as you live with the worldview of the sermon, you almost merge with the trail. You find that its rhythms are yours. It is not one thing among other things, but as near to your life as eating, drinking, sleeping, bathing . . . or not.

But why is it that even experienced hands get into the habit of the "day hike" or "sprint" sermon? Chalk it up to the usual suspects, including being too busy, or deferring the important and not urgent until tomorrow, or maybe a feeling that we can't do anything about something so far off. Additionally, I can hear my inner voice saying, "That ten-minute walk through a cemetery paid off last time, didn't it? And who knew? It's our secret. Don't worry about it, there's always a cemetery somewhere." My homiletical voice says, "Don't get used to that cemetery, because if you do, you may never leave it!" In the end, preaching isn't a day-hike or simply a sprinter's game. For some "weekend warriors" it may feel like a jump in and jump out sort of event but those who are yoked to the preaching life need something to fix their gaze for a larger purpose than simply "getting up a sermon" in time for Sunday. The Serenity Prayer comes to mind: "Grant me the serenity to accept the things I cannot change, the courage to change the things that I can, and the wisdom to know the difference." Another AA slogan feels relevant: "Just for today I will try to live through this day only, not tackling all of my problems at once. I can do something at this moment that would discourage me if I had to continue it for a lifetime." Doing "something" may fall well short of the sermon, but in other ways even that modest investment of energy pays for itself in the life of preaching. Below I present a sketch of how to keep the long view long while also keeping that initial plan for the sermon manageable.

Getting the Long View

I was asked to write a commentary on the season of Epiphany. My process was to go through each assigned text as it was listed for each Sunday. I simply followed the red thread of the texts, linking Old Testament readings to New Testament readings. When I had completed the commentary, which ended up being around eighty-five pages, I wrote the introduction. While the spade work of commenting on each set of lections was labor intensive, the synthesis, which came at the end, was relatively easy. I share this because preachers do the same thing, but our "synthesis" isn't something that comes at the "end," but rather leavens each encounter with the text. It builds, layer upon layer of interpretation. We can't go about it in the way I did with a commentary, researching and then, finally, just before the editor demands a manuscript, produce a well-rounded introduction. But the truth is that the best preaching contains a sense of the whole. This is what I mean when I say we, as preachers, begin to value the "long view" of the texts that we think about weekly.

At heart, to get the long view is to unfold the map of the preaching life and to think clearly about where you want to go. A red line on a map is something we consult in taking in the whole journey and as we break the path down into its natural lengths—is it an eight-mile day or a twenty-two-mile day? Are we going through an urban area or mountainous? How far apart are the places for rest and refreshment? The thing with homiletics is that it mostly (although not exclusively) equipped students for the sermon due in six weeks' time. In some ways, that is the concern of the church, at least on the surface. Yet when a minister looks at a parish or parishes, that person sees more than a sermon. They see learning opportunities, challenges, ideas that need fleshing out for congregational life, or aspects of the biblical imagination that have gone fallow. In the American context, new ministers might self-describe their style of preaching as pastoral, prophetic, or narrative, or topical, or perhaps doctrinal/expository. None of these, however, give you a sense of the specific learning opportunities within the congregation—that is the sort of thing that confronts us in our larger view of congregational formation.

Part Three: Community

You may identify, for instance, with a prophetic calling and think with that lens in your preaching—but what if you discover a basic absence of biblical and theological vocabulary in the congregation? If your preaching is all thunder and no lightning, that's not going to go very far for congregational development. If that is the case, choosing a teaching style, introducing the text as text (maybe before the sermon proper), helps the congregation achieve the theological and narrative location of the sermon. While it may seem like a small thing, a one-minute "teaching" on the text before reading the text acquaints everyone with how we're reading the map relative to the sermon itself.

Put another way, don't be a map hog. When Rebecca and I walk, if we quarrel, it's usually over who gets to read the map—and because we prefer marital bliss, we share the reading of the map, deciphering the way together. Congregational patterns of worship have liturgized the text into a ceremony rather than a piece of a longer journey, with a beginning, middle, and an end. What if we read Scripture and then basically said, "How do we read it in its historical situation (the teaching) and perhaps with a glimpse of how we might read it in ours (the preaching)?" Offer these teaching moments extempore or write them down and share them with the readers for the day's worship. The pattern of simply reading an ancient text and dropping us into the far country of Scripture feels less than satisfying—congregations benefit when the minister isn't a map hog.

In teaching, you know how it is: repetition builds familiarity and confidence with the text in hand. A teacherly approach emphasizes common themes in the narrative world of the Bible or perhaps explicitly notes a theme that recurs from Sunday to Sunday. As a style, it employs an iterative approach to the life with the sermon. In some parts of the Black preaching tradition, the preacher introduces a "theme" statement at the beginning of the sermon—this is more than a rhetorical device. It grounds the interpretive act in a summary or a distillation of the journey. Over time, this iterative approach recalls the previous Sunday and adds nuance through reiteration of the Sunday before that and the Sunday before that—and listeners begin to anticipate the next iteration of the theme. Like a palette of paint, a theme statement shows where we've been and, with the new blobs of paint, hints at the new space we'll explore in the next hour.

This points to a basic rule of thumb regarding how people listen: people never simply listen to what you say, they listen, guessing at what you *may* say—and sometimes vocalize what you *ought* to say. We may think that, as the primary speaker, we're charting the path but in fact our listeners are navigating already, guessing, or asking, "Where is this going?" Or, "This probably should go here..."

About a year into a ministry, I noted that while the congregation responded to "prophetic" sermons, they did not "get" the biblical narratives or the theology behind those sermons. As a result, I chose to take a teacherly approach with the Gospel of Matthew, reiterating patterns from Sunday to Sunday, borrowing the "theme" statement in the Black tradition of preaching, and offering a one- to two-minute "teaching" on the text before handing it over to the reader. By the end of that season of preaching, a person came up to me and remarked that she had learned to appreciate Matthew—it wasn't that she was uncritical of Matthew (she admitted that she had not "liked" Matthew's Gospel—think abusive landowners and so on), but because of this season of intentional teaching, Matthew's patterns grew in familiarity and even belonged with her experience of the Bible, as something named in a larger arc of biblical interpretation. She recognized the fingerprints of a Matthean Jesus! As a person, she still joined the marches and the neighborhood walks, but she did so with sensitivity to how Matthew's rule of the kingdom of heaven mapped onto the complicated legacies of kingdom-making of any kind.

Stalled, Abandoned, and Rediscovered

Artists seldom work only on one piece; they jam their studios with sketches and paintings at different levels of development, some stalled for years. I think artists share this in common with preachers: we all need purpose in our preaching, but the purpose needs to be larger than one work, one defining effort. No great achievement in art was ever the solo event of an artist's life. Van Gogh didn't wake up in the morning, take his palette to the south of France, and voila, produce *A Starry Night*. He crammed his palette with the colors that inspired him that day, but it also held the dry reminders of days past. In his studio, maybe we would find sketches that were still cooking in his imagination, pieces he started and abandoned, some that did not please him at first but later found them not only pleasing but almost revelatory. In the language of preachers, we talk about drafts and notes on texts and topics. Phillips Brooks wrote that he would often have a dozen or so different sermons in mind before he finally chose which sermon he would preach on Sunday. What happened to the other eleven? Saved for another day? Likely saved (written longhand in a notebook) rather than "deleted" as failed attempts. Brooks's approach, entertaining more than one or two possibilities, reflects what artists know instinctively: we're not creating something as such, but we are swept up in an intensely creative vocation. The sermon you choose for a Sunday is a symptom of the preaching life, not its culmination.

You may not have a dozen different sermon ideas competing for your attention, but you might have two or three or four hunches tickling your imagination. One of these you will select. The others you set to one side. Don't keep everything but don't throw it all away as the "darlings" you had to kill to find your sermon. That adage, to kill your darlings, gets over-extended to the point of actively unmaking the creative spirit. Keep your darlings, perhaps for another day. I print and revisit the 750 or 1,000 words of a rough draft for Sunday. I might use a third of that or maybe a paragraph for the "final" push to Sunday. However, the cuttings feel like things to revisit. You may be naming a problem that doesn't quite make the grade of "coherence" or the "direction of travel" for the Sunday coming, but in a way you're taking in the wider picture with associations and trajectories. Save these as hardcopy—it can include your edits for Sunday, but you want to preserve your work at least for your own digest. The pieces, fragments that seemed like false starts in the short run up to Sunday, may be better seen as different paths or ways which, on another week, may help you reinitiate a path that you didn't feel quite ready to take on before.

This suggests another kind of consideration: sometimes in our drafting, we tell our truth or truths. It may not be a truth we are prepared to share. It may be the sermon that we never share—and yet, in some way, that was the sermon that the Spirit preached to us, as a congregation of one. It may be that the "time" for sharing that truth is not right or fitting. We may say, "That's too much of personal self-disclosure. I'm not comfortable sharing that." Okay. At least give yourself permission to hear the sermon as it speaks to you, in your own awkward sense of place.

The sermon we live with borrows our body as its peculiar instrument, through which it sends its song. Listen for the song of the gospel in your life—you may hum it to yourself, or you may someday find the courage to sing it congregationally. That opportunity might not return to you again . . .

It was a sermon that was loosely based on the story of Jacob and Rebecca and the "seven years" of waiting that his father-in-law imposed on their marriage. The sermon was just before my son Gabriel's seventh birthday. I'd been in the congregation for two years at the time. Gabriel would ask, several times a day, when his birthday would be and we would tell him soon, very soon. It was the "music" in my life at the time. And it struck me as a way thinking about those seven years in the lives of Jacob and Rebecca—they may have seemed like seven thousand years or perhaps, quickened by love and passion, and looking back, it may have seemed like no time at all.

In form, the sermon was addressed directly to Gabriel but with the full awareness that the congregation would "overhear" this gospel. Gabriel did not necessarily get what was being said—his head would pop up from behind the pew whenever he heard me speak his name, but as soon as it passed his direct interest or comprehension, he returned to his nap or his coloring next to his mum. I spoke in a way that I would speak to a seven-year-old and yet with themes that he would only guess or partially understand—this was obvious as the "art" of the sermon. Indirectly, it became a way for all of us to enter a place where sometimes we simply won't go, how love changes time, changes us. Today, I would not preach this sermon—or perhaps ever again. Gabriel's a teenager now. That sermon, entitled "Seven Years Old," may never again sing congregationally, except in the odd hum of memory.

Perfecting the Deep Cast

I was an associate pastor, newly ordained. As a pattern for preaching, I chose my favorite text to preach from for my first sermon; and my next favorite for my second; and my third. By the time I got to my fourth sermon, I had run out of favorites. The Bible was too big, my inspiration too unpredictable, and my time was too short. I needed a plan. Preaching may find its lift and fun through inspiration, but to preach happily (not to say faithfully) we need to plan.

On the other end of that spectrum, Alistair Smeaton, a seasoned United Reformed Church minister in the UK (and an experienced Lake District hiker), posted a picture of four books from his personal library, each bound in that dirty red color popular with some of our religious presses. They were stacked on top of each other. At the bottom, a tattered, taped together hymnal; on top of it, another book with half the gold embossed lettering washed out, leaving a "Holy B" and for the rest, shadow; and *A Greek New Testament*, 4th rev. ed.; and, at the very top, another book of the same color, its markings completely faded—a Church of Scotland Book of Common

Prayer. "At a push," he writes, "I could do ministry with these four-color coordinated books."

Smeaton calls to mind what I call the skilled "deep cast" of the interpretive life: our deep books, prayers, and primary texts anchor the interpretive life or give it its weight, its potential depth. In fly fishing we practice the deep cast alongside the short cast. Whether deep or short, they have in common a basic law of physics: each cast uses the weight of the line and the flex of the pole to carry the fly to its destination out in the stream. For a long cast, especially, you need you be clear of obstacles behind you—it pays to think about the past as well as the future. The short cast, flicking the fly or the roll cast, are for close-up work but the long cast goes farther out. On a successful deep cast, where your fly lands may be shallow or near a pool, and you can't see if there are fish lurking beneath. It's really testing things out. As you get closer, you look for the shape of the trout, near the bottom, noses pointed into the current. And then your casts become more targeted. Occasionally, on a deep cast, you'll get a strike, mostly not. In a sense, you're thinking about the way forward, albeit through something that the trout might rise to rather than flee from.

A deep cast in preaching is the equivalent of planning out your preaching calendar as well as locating those texts that anchor your interpretive life. This is not less than choosing texts and it is more than choosing a text. You cast deep, but the line carries the fly. The line is weighted, so that you don't literally "throw" the fly. Light as a feather (literally) these lures don't get thrown. They get carried, as the line loops and rolls forward, its momentum carrying the tip to the target. You don't know what's up there, if anything. But knowing the line, how it loops and rolls, how it propels the feather light lure through the air to land as lightly as a breath on the water's surface, that's almost magic. For preachers, our preaching dates are, in essence, where we hope to present the fly. It's far off but not so far off as to be unimaginable.

But everything else is in the line, which means in the theological tradition, the liturgical season, the plan of readings. To make a deep cast with any kind of skill, you will need to shift your attention from your target to the skillful use of your tools. You don't need muscle but that awareness that the backstroke is ready to come forward, with the slight but firm bounce of the tip of your rod. Then almost like magic, you'll see your line sail over your head far ahead of you. Or you get tangled in an "obstacle" that you hadn't anticipated—in other words, looking forward means looking back simultaneously.

Distance Walking

At the risk of sounding insufficiently scholarly, those big tomes of biblical scholarship are probably the least helpful in an early stage of interpretation. For one, when you're planning far out, you're spreading out the map on the dining table, taking in some of the contour lines, the jogs south or north, east, or west; by contrast, biblical commentary mostly offers granular readings of specific texts. You will eventually join those readings but just not today.

Where then might you find the "weight" of the line? We might overlook two sources of interpretation that include wisdom from our tradition—our hymnody and prayers. It is odd that, of all our theological reading, our prayers and hymns seem to be easily passed over. "That person is a theologian who prays"—a saying from the Eastern Orthodox tradition—reminds us that theology belongs first to the person in prayer and only secondarily to the church or academy. Our daughter's math teacher invited parents to an evening session where he introduced us to what our children were learning, the different topics he would introduce as well as pedagogical approaches he used. At one of these meetings, he announced that schools had taken math away from children. I didn't know what that meant. Then he brought it home, telling us that when we saw our children using their fingers to do math problems, this was a good thing: math belongs to a child's body just as the arts belong to a child's imagination. Schools, he went on to explain, treat math as if it belongs to the school rather than to the lifeworld of children. He aimed to teach so that the principles of mathematics would always be understood as human capacities rather than academic impositions.

Something similar has happened to the theology of the church. Theology seems like a foreign word to many people in the church and yet our prayers, especially those in our hymns and liturgies, contain human capacities for theological reflection. Hymns and prayers do not replace exegetical reading, but they return the theological work of interpretation to the people who pray and sing. Begin early with the hymns, if not for the entire service, then as either responses to or preparation for the day's Scripture readings. We struggle to decipher Scripture when extracted from its context as worship and witness. When we hear it through the lens of prayer or song, we detect the sigh of God's Word to us.

Part Three: Community

Preaching Plans: Lectionary, Narrative, and Thematic

As you develop a long view of the preaching life, your first decision goes to the reading strategy. Will you follow the Revised Common Lectionary (RCL)? If so, will you be reading in a complementary way (finding the red thread connecting texts)? Or will you read in a semi-continuous way, following one book from Sunday to Sunday? Will you try a different kind of lectionary? Will you preach topically and find Scripture to explicate those topics? The prepared lectionary offers the least difficult plan for preaching. You don't have to look far for resources to support your worship planning. Hymns, prayers, commentary—it's out there in abundance, especially for the RCL. Below, I explore broad options for choosing our reading strategy.

Revised Common Lectionary and the Narrative Lectionary

The challenge of the RCL will not be finding resources but allowing yourself space to digest and process that rich cornucopia of interpretation. Otherwise, the resources available for lectionary preachers feels a bit like trying to drink from a fire hose. In fact, because publishers and websites produce such an abundance of material for the RCL, you need to get ownership of the text in your own way before leasing out the sermon moment to the "great" blog or homiletical equivalent of an "influencer"—instead choose a path that seems promising to you or just curious.

In a sense, the RCL selection of texts gives you a "day-hike" of the four lessons; the season (Christmas, Easter, or Ordinary Time); the year A, B, or C; and the three years A, B, and C. For the big picture, do a comparative reading of the years A, B, and C. You might even look at what has been omitted from A, B, C and then added in a proposed Year D (this idea is really part of a sense of unrest with the RCL broadly—more on that below).

If you're planning is more modest, begin by doing an initial dig into the text at least four or five weeks in advance. Even better, read through the three major cycles of the Christian calendar and work on each. If that's too much, choose a "culmination" Sunday that gives you a big enough bite of text, maybe in Lent looking at Pentecost Sunday for the Easter cycle and work backwards. This achieves two goals: one is that it gets you thinking further out (procrastination nipped in the bud), and it also helps you to think theologically and eschatologically about the trajectory of resurrection without you trying too hard. That we think from the "end" of the story is axiomatic among theologians—but those of us who live with sermons preach from the beginning of the season. Some might point out that, for example, Advent texts begin with apocalyptic texts that signal the "ending" complexion of the Christmas season. That supplies a clue to how we understand incarnation but, as teachers, having its significance clearly in mind gives us a framework for apocalyptic readings.

Scholarly support needs to be solid and, most of all, accessible. Now is not the time for a *Hermeneutica-* or even *Anchor Bible*-style commentary (unless you're simply looking at the commentator's translation). A single volume like *Harper's* or *New Interpreter's Bible* on your desk should be more than enough. Bible open; commentary (brief entries for each text); notepad for you. *Working Preacher* has, over the years, acquired an impressive archive of materials. Commentary is usually just about one thousand words, or about six minutes reading time. Write down a sentence or two that comes out of that exercise, set it aside in your planning journal, and go on to the "urgent and important" cluster of things that to be finished: getting Advent readers organized, sending out the congregational letter, sitting down with staff to go over the week's work, carrying out pastoral care.

Relatively more recent to the scene is the Narrative Lectionary (NL), a four-year cycle of readings.[1] If you were to choose the NL, that would be a different kind of journey than the one mapped by the RCL. The NL blends the Reformed Tradition's preference for *lectio continua*, or ongoing reading of the Bible with texts that tell the story of God's saving love. This reflects a change from the RCL insofar that the NL, while still including the cycles of the Christian year, emphasizes the story of God through the pages of the Bible. By contrast, in the RCL a christocentric pattern, coming from its rootage in the theology of the mass, governs the lessons. Ordinary Time, the third major cycle of readings in the RCL, is your one opportunity for truly semi-continuous readings of either Old Testament or New Testament texts, decoupled from the christocentricity of Christmas and Easter.

As an alternative to the RCL, the developers of the NL identify a theology of God within the readings alongside a preference for the narrative dynamic of Scripture:

> Texts were selected that lead well to the proclamation of what God is doing. The stories tell of hope and disappointment, suffering and redemption. In all these varied contexts, we find God dealing with the complexities of human life. Stories from the gospels differ

1. See *Working Preacher*, "What is the Narrative Lectionary?"

each year, avoiding repetition and highlighting what is distinctive about each gospel's telling of the story of Jesus.[2]

The developers of the NL have not taken leave of the lectionary calendar, particularly its Christmas and Easter cycles (and have thus preserved the christological depth of the RCL), but they have designed it for preachers and congregations that can be expected to digest just one Scripture lesson on a Sunday rather than the four lessons associated with the RCL. By doing so, the NL evidences a preferential option for the kind of preaching that the Reformed tradition was built on as well as the view that most of us relate our faith and lives through narratives. It also says something about the task of preaching: when we try to "pair" four lessons we may get the big picture but never the odd spirit of one of the lessons, as it speaks in its own way. The NL, moreover, begins to answer a desire for a diversity of reading strategies, as something of an antidote to LFS (Lectionary Fatigue Syndrome), which is sometimes associated with the RCL. Again, thinking about this from the perspective of congregations and ministers who have, at least historically, known biblical interpretation as a keystone part of their identity, the NL provides a needed corrective.

The NL also hints at a concept that we touched on earlier, the idea of a theme statement. A theme statement or controlling idea offers a map of where we are, a continent or a region. An extended lesson of Scripture details what that might look like in terms of our navigation of that larger theme. With that kind of scoping in mind, the NL includes two readings, a preaching text (ranging anywhere from ten or so verses to around twenty), and an "accompanying reading" which, according to the NL, is optional (usually very short, one or maybe three verses). Optional or not, this accompanying text thematizes without narrative explanation to further refine its meaning within its narrative context—that decision leads the interpreter to the longer preaching text as it works out the principle or idea implicit in the accompanying reading.

So, for example, in Year One, for the Fourteenth Sunday after Pentecost, the NL lists Matthew 8:24–27, the story of Jesus calming the storm, to accompany the preaching text, the flood story of Genesis (6:5–22; 8:6–12; 9:8–17). As interpreters, the idea of Jesus' power to "still troubled waters" is overly brief, not being substantial enough in terms of cut to sustain a sermon. But that's really the point: it only points in the direction we're going but it doesn't narrate the path itself. For listeners, the short narrative of

---

2. *Working Preacher*, "What is the Narrative Lectionary?"

Jesus evokes (but does not situate into a larger narrative) deep memories of their own journey of faith. The NL helpfully turns our interpretive energy and our christological leanings into the Genesis story, allowing us to go deeper into the Old Testament world. Similarly, for the Seventh Sunday of Easter, the NL lists Jesus' brief saying about no one being able to serve two masters (Matt 6:24) as the accompanying text—a conceptual text it says nothing about the christological allegiance implicit in the church's understanding of Jesus' lordship or Matthew's view of Jesus as alternative to the Roman Empire—instead, for this, you get Paul in Romans 6:1–14. This pairing by the NL gives anyone who has ever wondered "how" to relate Paul's Christology to the Jesus of the Gospels a fresh challenge and a new insight into Jesus' situation in a Roman imperial context. In Paul we hear that our baptism is a form of allegiance, and we are called to "activate" that allegiance amid powers that compete for our loyalty. In effect, by extracting the question of allegiance from Matthew, the interpreter can then look closely at Paul's thinking as an evocation of what it means for people of faith today to activate their allegiance to Christ in the world.

Topical Light

"Preaching in the age of Trump is no picnic," says Agnes W. Norflect, pastor of Bryn Mawr Presbyterian Church, Bryn Mawr, Pennsylvania. After thirty years of preaching, of following Barth's dictum of holding a newspaper in one hand and the Bible in the other, of earned expertise in the interpretation of Scripture, work with scholarly commentary and theological resources, she believes we are now in a different place: "These three decades have seen the multiple crises of rising urban homelessness, tsunamis and hurricanes, famines across continents, migrations of refugees, escalating gun violence, the frightening degradation of the environment, and the increasingly voluminous #MeToo movement.... We need a different kind of help now. We need more guidance exegeting current movements and social institutions to figure out what is happening in a rapidly changing cultural and political milieu."[3]

This is one of those areas where, in my teaching of homiletics, I simply didn't spend a lot of time. We all lived in the post-Barth world, otherwise known to have inaugurated a turn to biblical preaching and then, later to narrative approaches. It's also an age that, at least in the academy,

3. Norflect, "One New Book for the Preacher," 45.

was exhausted with the liberal project of translation, correlating biblical truths with their modern and scientific counterparts, e.g., translating the life of the soul into categories of psychology. I was dismissive of thematic approaches to preaching in part for this reason, among others. More importantly, I held to the notion that thematic preaching may be relevant, but it is not revelatory. When pastors choose themes rather than texts, we strap the Word into backseat, perhaps into the child's seat, while we make the important decisions about where we're going and how fast and why or to what end. Today, I hear loud and clear Norflect's concern for guidance in preaching on thematic questions.

What, for example, do you say on the Sunday following the Pulse shootings? Or the Tree of Life Synagogue shootings? Or the Charleston AME shooting? Or as your community tries to rebuild after its second thousand-year flood in less than five years? When we preach in those times, there is a kind of focus to our efforts. We call it the crisis sermon because the crisis acts as the primary catalyst, activating all our theological and interpretive skills with an urgent request. A crisis sermon is a topical sermon that addresses some national or local tragedy. But what if the whole fabric of society is being rent and torn and it's not a crisis once or twice a year, but an ongoing crisis, perhaps like the climate crisis? As one climatologist noted, we've gone from predicting what will happen when climate change arrives, to describing what just happened in the aftermath of its arrival. Or perhaps a significant portion of our congregation would live in happy denial, ignoring the phenomenon of whiteness while at the same time benefiting from whiteness and being horrified by those who espouse White nationalism. We need a different kind of help now.

On one level, this type of preaching asks interpreters to move in different circles than they're accustomed to moving. It's not that texts, commentary, and theological resources are not important—they are—but we must be honest: the status quo which we've railed against in our prophetic moments is crumbling around us and far from being happy about it, most of us are alarmed. Based on the news cycle, you could almost justify preaching topically *every* Lord's Day. Perhaps that wouldn't be altogether bad. But that's not your only option. Typically, topical preaching means the careful explication of a public concern within a theological framework with a call to some kind of faithful response. However, if we expand our horizon from The Sermon which addresses A Crisis for All Time to a season of crisis preaching, we might move to what I call a thematic-light mode. In

Distance Walking

a thematic-light mode, interpreters take an ongoing crisis as a minor key for every sermon. It's more like a covenant than an exegetical exercise, or perhaps a commitment of attentiveness to a specific public concern.

One of the reasons (though obviously not the only one) that congregations feel that their preachers are too political is because they are not political often enough. Which is to say, congregations in the mainline tradition have been formed in a tradition of reading Scripture without political implications. If we signal that politics is not far off in our preaching effort, even when a public question is not the presenting issue of the sermon, we may prepare the congregation for those seasons in church life where the call to reflect (and take sides) is much steeper. There's another distinction: as those who preach, we ought to avoid "playing" politics, but we are called to "do" justice, to make justice, build and foster the conditions for justice.

Today's crises have created a sense of hopelessness, or cynicism, or sometimes simply denial. This is where we preach. Or we preach as antidote for a world in which, according to Norflect, "'faith seeking understanding' seems to have morphed into 'despair clinging to a modicum of hope.'"[4] It may also be a sermon to create disturbance where there is complacency. Linda Martin Alcoff begins her oddly hopeful work on *The Future of Whiteness* with this sentence: "This is a book about a topic many would rather avoid. That topic is white identity, its difficult past, complicated future, and uncertain future."[5] How would those words, slightly revised, sound on Sunday morning? The introduction to a sermon series on the topic of whiteness in today's America, in our congregations?

A couple of things to remember in this kind of preaching: you are entering a conversation where you are not the authority. In a way, that's familiar territory for preachers who, week in and week out, stray into ancient history, on a mission to salvage something for a congregation on Sunday. On the other hand, when we wade deep into questions of race and identity in America, we're not umpires of truth but rather co-conspirators with God in a journey towards God's reconciliation and repair.

But this sort of modesty in our role as preachers isn't the same as vanishing. My very first "social issues" sermon was on the topic of the arson committed against Black churches in South Carolina. It was 1995. I preached a sermon in which, quite dramatically, I said that if the KKK was going to destroy churches, well, we would rebuild them. We sang "Amazing

---

4. Norflect, "One New Book for the Preacher," 45.
5. Alcoff, *Future of Whiteness*, 1.

Grace," I gave the charge and benediction, and people filed out into the afternoon. But one person asked me a question that I was stumped by: "What do we do? I want to respond, but I don't know how." A sermon in this key has a practical dimension; it's not all soaring rhetoric. It entails how we will live in a world where the high moral octane of the sermonic "ought" exists in tension with the complicated, messy, often unpredictable "is" of contemporary social ferment.

Textual Harassment

At one time, preachers chose texts to "ravish" the congregation with the expansive promise of God's love and presence. There's still a place for that kind of thematic preaching. But I'm also struck by texts of terror—or some version of textual harassment. That is, consider choosing texts that are difficult, or texts of harassment, as your key preaching texts. This is kind of a hybrid-topical/textual sermon because a "text of terror" is often terrorizing in the sense that it seems to espouse something we have firmly and flatly rejected. This may be the "wives submit to your husband" sort of text or texts that admonish people in slavery to "obey your masters"—Frances Taylor Gench, speaking as a feminist scholar, says these are examples of "textual harassment." Gench argues that most mainline pulpits pass these texts over in silence to their own harm. When we choose to pass over difficult texts in silence, others will give voice to those texts in ways that undermine progressive and inclusive societies.[6] The same is true for the book of Revelation. Mainline pastors often won't touch Revelation and, as a result, leave it to anti-Semites, White nationalists, and others. Even concluding that we reject the values or the social world envisioned by the writer is, in a way, to be edified through the reading of difficult texts. This is not an unusual lesson. Sometimes, we read difficult texts, not because we enjoy difficult, thorny issues but because those conversations, which make us shift uncomfortably in our pew, exercise our intellectual faculties.

---

6. See Gench, *Encountering God in Tyrannical Texts*.

Distance Walking

Signposts: Sewing Spirit Beads into the Leather of Our Work

Artists in First Nations traditions weave into everything a mistake, not as a slip, but as an intention, as a proclamation of who we are this side of Eden. Brenda Mahan, my Athabascan cousin, explains the imperfection with a wristband in which she made use of porcupine quills—porcupine quills are delicate and require great skill in quillwork. She says my wristband was her "very first attempt at this type of quillwork." She continues:

> As you can see, it is not perfect. We are taught that we are not perfect, only the Creator is—therefore our pieces cannot be perfect. Some people put a spirit bead in their pieces (to make them imperfect), but I like my spirit bead to "happen naturally." When beads are put into the tubes, sometimes a different color bead sneaks in and I call that a natural spirit bead.

Brenda points to the spirituality that permeates the work—it is not the idolatry of a thing but the testimony of a human response, giving human shape to the Creator's beauty.

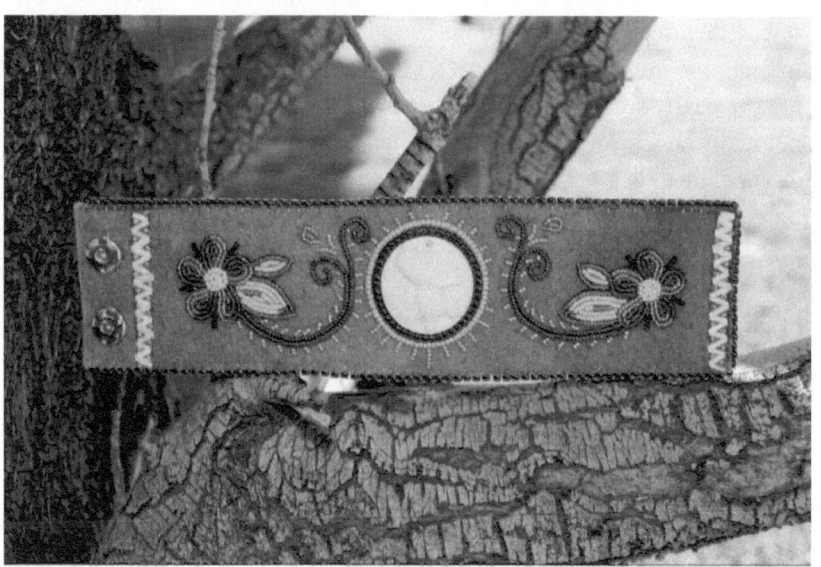

Part Three: Community

I sometimes study her work, trying to "see" with my own eye the spirit bead. So far, I haven't found it. But when I think critically about my own preaching, finding that spirit bead is easy and hard at the same time. The presence of the spirit bead is not initially a blessing, at least to my eye. Maybe for those of us who preach, we need someone else to see the spirit bead, to help us appreciate its creative significance. I'm thinking here of the role of pastoral coaching or the coaching that we might hear from people who may have lived with the sermon in their own journey. This is not to say anyone needs a homiletician as a coach, but we may need someone who understands the life of the preacher and knows the tender parts of the human condition in the way a therapist or a wise coach might. In one session with my coach, I shared a sermon that didn't go as well as I'd hoped. It was a new area for me as a preacher and I was clumsy. When I shared my disappointment in myself, she might have heard me despairing of my vocation entirely. She took a quick look at my mistake and saw it for it was: "You were in the arena!" All I could see was the mistake, vast, ugly, and all-consuming; but what she helped me to see was the witness to something bigger than me. She saw the spirit in the bead of peculiar color.

Jonathan Sacks wrote about leaders, especially moral leaders. He was a rabbi and moral philosopher; he wrote for a popular audience but he would understand the pastor's life, particularly as leadership. Peril as well as blindness haunts the leader. They are not able, from their talent and resources, to rescue themselves from situations larger and more complex than they are. In *Morality: Restoring the Common Good in Divided Times*, Sacks recounts how he nearly drowned during his honeymoon on the coast in Italy. He did not know how to swim, but seeing others standing farther out from shore, he concluded that it was safe to simply walk out into water that only came up to their knees. Sacks went into the water, wading to where he had seen people a few minutes before. Then he turned back:

> That's when it happened. Within a minute I found myself out of my depth. How it happened, I'm not sure. There must have been a dip in the sand. I had missed it on my way out but on my way back I had walked straight into it. I tried to swim. I failed. I kept going under . . . I was sure this was the end. As I went under for the fifth time, I remember thinking two thoughts. "What a way to begin a honeymoon." And, "What is Italian for 'Help'?" . . . I had already reconciled myself to drowning when someone, seeing me thrashing about, swam over, took of hold of me, and brought me to the shore.

Distance Walking

Sacks says that, for him, this experience speaks to the limits of the self-help genre and to the profound nature of real rescue: "Help, I have found time and again, comes not from the self, but from others."[7]

He lists half a dozen leaders and their coaches or muses, many of whom were never seen except in the autobiography that came long after their retirement from public life. However, he claims that when that muse dropped out of the orbit of the leader, their skills suffered as a result. "There is usually someone empowered to whisper in their ear and say No. A leader cannot be *in* the fray and *above* it at the same time."[8] Maybe the art of seeing the spirit bead, the yes and the no, as bead *and* spirit, seeing the error and also the way of rescue, belongs not to you, but to a companion who has walked a path like but not identical to your own. We may enter ministry almost in the spirit of a solo, but the longer we live with the sermon and its path, the more we need the eyes of the other.

Our human shape cannot be perfect. Into each sermon weave a spirit bead, a bead of a different color or a different hue sown directly into the sermonic leather, that can only be explained as an imperfection or open sign, as testimony to the Creator. What would our preaching be like if every sermon prayed for the gift of imperfection, looked for it? How will we sow our "spirit beads" into the leather of our lives, the skins of our work, as people who live with sermons? And who will teach us to see them and even ourselves as the imperfect pairing of spirit and bead, testifying to Creator?

---

7. Sacks, *Morality*, 38–39.
8. Sacks, *Morality*, 43.

Conclusion
Beyond the Lonely Planet

"But in the end, stories are about one person saying to another: This is the way it feels to me. Can you understand what I'm saying? Does it feel this way to you?"

—Kazuo Ishiguro

OVER THE COURSE OF this book, we have experienced something of the "peek and wink" of the preaching life. Each chapter included my stories. They're me asking you, "Does it feel this way to you?" I think about that silver-haired gentlemen on the footpath in the middle of the North Yorkshire Moors, sitting with his "cuppa." It felt natural to talk with him and he was happy to talk with us. It wasn't a long conversation. Maybe five minutes. That's what I've tried to do in this meditation on the preaching life, five minutes here and there, and maybe they will linger with you, too. I identify with that stranger. Over the last decade, I've gotten grayer a lot sooner than I had hoped. Maybe this book is something like that person sitting there, thinking about the footpath, resting between steps. Perhaps he is wondering about the strangers coming his way—guessing, as they got closer, where they are going, intimating what they are feeling, maybe what they need at that moment, not too much, not too little. He might have got it wrong. As it happens, he got us just about right.

Doesn't always happen that way. Sometimes, the person you meet on the footpath isn't really giving you what you need but rather satisfying some need they have in themselves. On the Cumbria Way, we were slowly making our way towards Great Langdale from Coniston. We were a bit puzzled

Conclusion

by a tangle of intersecting footpaths and wondering whether we had perhaps missed the way. I asked another hiker whether we were on the way to Great Langdale. I'd only wanted a left or right level of clarification. He went on to give us a long lecture, finally telling us that for us "it was going to be a *long* day." Giving us a quick once over, he added that there was an ice cream truck down the road. He became a bit of an inside joke, every time we felt a bit tired or frustrated, "It's going to be a *long* day!" Or "Don't worry, there's an ice cream truck waiting for us at the trig point!" He wasn't helpful but he added some inside humor to the walk. I hope you will have found this book to be mostly on the side of some companionable advice. Whatever my advice, it was only what I had to offer. You're under no obligation to take any of it. Of course, if you're feeling tired, and it's been a long day, there's an ice cream truck not too far ahead . . .

Whatever else you take from this book, I hope it helps with navigation and with what it might mean to get close to the edge of the map—or to take leave of the map entirely. In the end, go deep, go where the maps fail or grow dim. Like a walking guide, this one pales in comparison to the journey itself: by comparison to the wilderness around you, or the sound of real, living waters, the way sometimes the Spirit speaks in hushed murmurs and silences; or to the moment of crossing a continental divide of interpretation, where suddenly you discover interpretation breaking away dramatically, in another and perhaps unanticipated direction; or the thrill (and terror) of the preaching moment, as words toddle forth, awkward, sometimes childlike, prophetic in their simplicity, folly to the world but the power of salvation to those who believe—by comparison to the lived experience, a book like this will always be regarded as commentary or an interesting footnote.

After Rebecca and I finish a walk, we sometimes talk about framing the map, showing the marks of the actual road, its otherwise "objective" marks torn and creased by use in rain and wind.

We never have. Is it something in us that to memorialize a map would be wrong somehow, betraying its humble existence? Is it simply that this thing was for a time, a cloak of contour lines and footpaths, a compass that gave us north in a heavy mist, a stranger who told us where to find the Lion Inn, how it would be when we first saw it?

"You won't miss it," he said. "It'll peek at you and then it'll wink away."

Bibliography

Alcoff, Linda Martín. *The Future of Whiteness*. Cambridge: Polity, 2015.
American Psychological Association. "Trigger." https://dictionary.apa.org/trigger.
Anderson, Laurie. "Big Science: Walking and Falling." Nonesuch Records, 2007. https://www.youtube.com/watch?v=gxeK-KYvibc.
Auerbach, Frank. "Letter to Glasgow Museum." August 2, 2015.
Barreto, Eric. "Commentary on Matthew 5:21–37." February 16, 2020. https://www.workingpreacher.org/commentaries/revised-common-lectionary/sixth-sunday-after-epiphany/commentary-on-matthew-521-37-4 on June 16, 2023.
Bell, Susan. *The Artful Edit: On the Practice of Editing Yourself*. New York: W. W. Norton and Company, 2007.
Berry, Wendell. *The Unforeseen Wilderness: Kentucky's Red River Gorge*. Emeryville, CA: Shoemaker & Hoard, 1991.
Blower, David Benjamin, and Nicholas Postlethwaite. "Changed by the Margins." Episode 5, *Common Era: Spirituality in an Age of Change*. https://www.youtube.com/watch?v=WXfweTQL7p0&list=PL2Q5N2DVZNs1djvmqiHrximSpotZUARWD&index=12.
Bonhoeffer, Dietrich. "Letter to Julie Bonhoeffer, August 20, 1933." Excerpted in Bernd Wannenwetsch, "Bonhoeffer and the War over Disabled Life," in *Disability in the Christian Tradition,* edited by Brian Brock and John Swinton, 370–71. Grand Rapids: Eerdmans, 2012.
———. *Letters and Papers from Prison*. Edited by Victoria J. Barnett and Barbara Wojhoski. Dietrich Bonhoeffer Works 8. Minneapolis: Fortress, 2010.
———. *Prayerbook of the Bible*. Edited by Wayne Whitson Floyd, Jr. Dietrich Bonhoeffer Works 5. Minneapolis: Fortress, 2005.
Brueggemann, Walter. *The Message of the Psalms: A Theological Commentary*. Minneapolis: Augsburg, 1984.
———. *The Psalms and the Life of Faith*. Edited by Patrick D. Miller. Minneapolis: Fortress, 1995.
Campbell, Edward F. Jr. *Ruth: A New Translation with Introduction and Commentary*. The Anchor Yale Bible. New Haven: Yale University Press, 1975.
Canadian Museum of History. "Tsimshian Mask." https://www.historymuseum.ca/cmc/exhibitions/tresors/treasure/225eng.html.

Bibliography

Coffey, Sarah. "Prosthesis." University of Chicago. http://csmt.uchicago.edu/glossary2004/prosthesis.htm.

Dillard, Annie. *The Writing Life*. New York: Harper & Row, 1989.

Eiesland, Nancy L. *The Disabled God: Toward a Liberation Theology of Disability*. Nashville: Abingdon, 1994.

First Nations Version: An Indigenous Translation of the New Testament. Downers Grove, IL: InterVarsity, 2021.

Flintoff, John-Paul. *Psalms for the City*. Kindle ed. London: SPCK, 2022.

Gench, Frances Taylor. *Encountering God in Tyrannical Texts: Reflections on Paul, Women, and the Authority of Scripture*. Louisville: Westminster John Knox, 2015.

Harris, James. *Preaching Liberation*. Minneapolis: Fortress, 1995.

Hawkins, Kathleen. "Two Disabled Men." *BBC*, April 18, 2015. https://www.bbc.co.uk/news/blogs-ouch-32315809.

Hoch, Robert. "Gaining Perspective: Getting in Touch with Your Inner Homiletician." *Working Preacher*, April 21, 2015. https://www.workingpreacher.org/sermon-development/gaining-perspective-getting-in-touch-with-your-inner-homiletician-part-2.

———. "A Peculiar Instinct." In *From Hope to Wholeness: A Presbyterian Response to the Unrest in Baltimore in April 2015*, edited by John V. Carlson et al., 98–106. Cleveland: Parson's Porch, 2016.

———. "Podcast with Dr Anthony Reddie." March 2023. https://nwsynod.org.uk/wp-content/uploads/2023/02/Rob-Hoch-23022023.m4a.

———. "Yet You Shall Be Different." In the Voices (online) section of the *The Presbyterian Outlook*, July 3, 2015. https://pres-outlook.org/2015/07/yet-you-shall-be-different/.

Hoke, Chris. *Wanted: A Spiritual Pursuit Through Jail, Among Outlaws, and Across Borders*. New York: Harper Collins, 2015.

Koyama, Kosuke. *Three Mile an Hour God*. London: SCM, 2015.

Lee, Sang Hyun. *From a Liminal Place: An Asian American Theology*. Minneapolis: Fortress, 2010.

Lowry, Eugene. *The Homiletical Plot: The Sermon as Narrative Art Form*. Expanded ed. Louisville: Westminster John Knox, 2000.

Neruda, Pablo. *Extravagaria*. Translated by Alastair Reid. London: Jonathan Cape, 1972.

Norflect, Agnes W. "One New Book for the Preacher." *Journal for Preachers* 42, no. 2 (Lent 2019) 45–47.

Pew Research Center. "Choosing a New Church or House of Worship." https://www.pewresearch.org/religion/2016/08/23/1-the-search-for-a-new-congregation/.

Ponte, Katharine. "Understanding Mental Illness Triggers." January 10, 2022. https://www.nami.org/Blogs/NAMI-Blog/January-2022/Understanding-Mental-Illness-Triggers.

Proctor, Samuel. *The Certain Sound of the Trumpet: Crafting a Sermon of Authority*. Prussia: Judson, 1994.

Reddie, Anthony G. *Is God Color Blind? Insights from Black Theology for Christian Faith and Ministry*. 2nd ed. London: SPCK, 2020.

———. *Theologising Brexit: A Liberationist and Postcolonial Critique*. London: Routledge, 2019.

Sacks, Jonathan. *Morality: Restoring the Common Good in Divided Times*. London: Hodder and Stoughton, 2020.

Sakenfeld, Katharine Doob. *Ruth: A Bible Commentary for Teaching and Preaching*. Interpretation. Louisville: Westminster John Knox, 1999.

Bibliography

Schipper, Jeremy. *Ruth: A New Translation with Introduction and Commentary.* The Anchor Yale Bible 7d. New Haven: Yale University Press, 2016.
Smith, Iman. "Content Notice: Here Are A Few Ways Professors Use Trigger Warnings." National Public Radio, September 21, 2016. https://www.npr.org/sections/codeswitch/2016/09/21/493913099/content-notice-here-are-a-few-ways-professors-use-trigger-warnings.
Smith, James K. A. "Obliqueness and Extravagance: A Conversation with Rowan Williams and Shane McCrae." *Image* 115 (Winter 2022) 55–64.
———. "Of God and Monsters." In "A Tree, a Rock, and Cloud: Curation, Criticism, and Commentary," *Image* (June 3, 2023). https://mailchi.mp/imagejournal.org/jamienewsletter-2023-june-633857.
Usher, Graham B. *The Way Under Our Feet: A Spirituality of Walking.* London: SPCK, 2020.
Wainwright, A. *Coast to Coast: From St. Bees Head to Robin Hood's Bay.* Kendal: Westmorland Gazette, 1973.
Weston, Ruth. Unpublished Manuscript.
Weil, Simone. *Gravity and Grace.* Translated by Gustave Thibon. London: Routledge and Kegan Paul, 1952.
Willett, Mischa. "Shape-Shifter: The Native American Iconography of Preston Singletary." *Image* 116 (Spring 2023) 34–43.
Winnicott, D. W. *Playing and Reality.* London: Routledge, 1982.
Working Preacher. "What is the Narrative Lectionary?" https://www.workingpreacher.org/narrative-faq.

www.ingramcontent.com/pod-product-compliance
Lightning Source LLC
Chambersburg PA
CBHW030856170426
43193CB00009BA/636